POKéMON
Pathways to Adventure

Jason R. Rich

SYBEX San Francisco • Paris • Düsseldorf • Soest • London

Official Nintendo Licensed Product

Associate Publisher	ROGER STEWART
Contracts and Licensing Manager	KRISTINE PLACHY
Acquisitions and Publications Manager	DAN BRODNITZ
Managing Editor Game Books	TORY McLEARN
Editor	LAURA ARENDAL
Production Editor and Proofreader	KARI BROOKS
Book Design	VAN WINKLE DESIGN GROUP
Book Production	WILLIAM SALIT DESIGN
Production Assistant	LISA LUSK
Cover Designer	CALYX DESIGN

SYBEX is a registered trademark of SYBEX Inc.

Pathways to Adventure is a trademark of SYBEX Inc.

Pokémon™ Nintendo® and character names are trademarks of Nintendo of America Inc. 1995, 1996 and 1998 Nintendo, CREATURES, GAME FREAK. ™ and ® are trademarks of Nintendo. ©1999 Nintendo

TRADEMARKS: SYBEX has attempted throughout this book to distinguish proprietary trademarks from descriptive terms by following the capitalization style used by the manufacturer.

The author and publisher have made their best efforts to prepare this book. The author and the publisher make no representation or warranties of any kind with regard to the completeness or accuracy of the contents herein and accept no liability of any kind including but not limited to performance, merchantability, fitness for any particular purpose, or any losses or damages of any kind caused or alleged to be caused directly or indirectly from this book.

Copyright ©1999 SYBEX Inc., 1151 Marina Village Parkway, Alameda, CA 94501. World rights reserved. No part of this publication may be stored in a retrieval system, transmitted, or reproduced in any way, including but not limited to photocopy, photograph, magnetic or other record, without the prior agreement and written permission of the publisher.

Library of Congress Card Number: 98-89150

ISBN: 0-7821-2503-4

Manufactured in the United States of America

10 9 8 7 6 5 4

To everyone at Creatures, Inc., Game Freak, Inc., and Nintendo who were responsible for creating the Pokémon game and making it an incredible phenomenon throughout the world!

Acknowledgments

Thanks once again to Roger Stewart and Dan Brodnitz at Sybex for approving the Pathways to Adventure concept and allowing me to work on this book. I'd also like to thank Laura Arendal, Tory McLearn, Senoria Bilbo-Brown, William Salit, and Kari Brooks at Sybex for all of their efforts, working under a tight deadline, to publish this book.

Without the assistance of Susan Eisner and Susan Simpson at Leisure Concepts, as well as the folks in Nintendo of America's licensing department—including Juana Tingdale, Ellen Enrico, and Cammy Budd—this book would not have been possible.

I'd also like to thank Howard Lincoln, Peter Main, George Harrison, Perrin Kaplan, Beth Llewelyn, Scott Pelland, and Gail Tilden from Nintendo of America for their ongoing support.

My sincere gratitude also goes out to my family and two closest and dearest friends, Mark Giordani and Ellen Bromfield, for their never-ending love and support!

Finally, thanks to you, the reader. I hope you find reading Pokémon: Pathways to Adventure as exciting as playing the Nintendo Game Boy game itself.

Jason R. Rich

http://www.jasonrich.com

Contents

CHAPTER 1
Ash Meets his First Pokémon ...1

CHAPTER 2
Ash Expands his Pokémon Collection ...13

CHAPTER 3
Ash Visits the Pewter City Gym ...23

CHAPTER 4
The Journey to Cerulean City and Beyond ...31

CHAPTER 5
All Aboard! ...45

CHAPTER 6
Fun 'n' Games Within Celadon City ...57

CHAPTER 7
Team Rocket Invades Saffron City ...69

CHAPTER 8
Hunting Season at the Safari Zone ...79

CHAPTER 9
A True Pokémon Master in the Making ...91

Pathways to Adventure

Introduction

Do you love competing at sports, playing video games, or hanging out with your friends? Then you must be a teenager from Earth. If you were a young person living in the World of Pokémon, you would spend nearly all your free time doing something completely different—raising and training Pokémon and entering them into competitions!

What? You don't know what a Pokémon is?

These wonderful creatures live in the wild; they are small but very powerful. Some people catch Pokémon and raise them as pets, but most train them to compete with other Pokémon. There are more than 150 different kinds of Pokémon, each with its own abilities and special powers. These creatures are intelligent, distinctive, and are very loyal to their trainers if raised properly. Just about everyone hopes to become a great Pokémon Master, a title that only a very few of the best trainers are able to achieve.

This is the story of one brave boy named Ash. He is one of many young people in Pallet Town, a small town in the World of Pokémon. More than anything, Ash wants to someday become a Pokémon Master and collect all the different types of Pokémon.

For his whole life, Ash has lived next door to a boy named Gary. Ash and Gary have been rivals for eleven years—ever since they were very young. But they really have a lot in common: both want to become the world's greatest Pokémon Master.

Gary's grandfather, Professor Oak, is a widely respected Pokémon expert. Because of his years of experience in training and studying Pokémon, people call him the "Pokémon Prof." An extremely smart and kind man, Professor Oak offers training tips and guidance to all the Pokémon trainers in Pallet Town.

At this point in his young life, Ash has already read all sorts of Pokémon books, magazines, and training manuals, preparing for the day when he would finally begin his collection and work toward making his dreams and goals come true.

As our story begins, Ash is about to enter a world of dreams and adventures, where his very own Pokémon legend will unfold...

Pathways to Adventure

Pokémon

CHAPTER 1

Ash Meets His First Pokémon

Ash had spent an action-packed morning playing Super NES video games in his bedroom, but it was time to get going, so he went downstairs. Spotting his mother at the table, he walked over to her. "Professor Oak next door is looking for you," she told him.

Full of energy, Ash ran out of his house in search of the Pokémon Prof. First he tried Gary's house, right next door. But Ash only found the professor's pretty young granddaughter—Gary's sister—at home. "Hi Ash!" she said. "Gary is out at Grandpa's lab."

Perhaps Professor Oak was there, too!

Ash knew exactly where the Oak Pokémon Research Lab was—it was near Gary's house. When he got there, he ran straight to the back of the building.

But instead of the Prof, he found his rival, Professor Oak's grandson Gary. "Yo Ash—Gramps isn't around," said Gary. Disappointed that the Professor was nowhere around, Ash decided to exit the lab and continue his search. In the lab, however, he noticed three Poké Balls on the lab table, each containing a different Pokémon.

After searching Pallet Town, Ash decided the professor must have left town, so he headed up toward the route to Viridian City. Just as he got to the beginning of the path, he heard a shout: "Hey! Wait! Don't go out!"

Turning around, Ash saw Professor Oak running toward him. "It's unsafe! Wild Pokémon live in tall grass! You need your own Pokémon for your protection," warned the professor. "I know! Come with me." Excited, Ash followed the professor back toward the lab.

Pathways to Adventure

When they got to the building, Gary was still waiting in the back of the lab. Professor Oak had summoned him earlier, but by now, Gary was feeling very impatient. "Gramps! I'm fed up with waiting!" he said. But Professor Oak would not be rushed.

 "Wild Pokémon live in tall grass! You need your own Pokémon for your protection!"

The professor turned to Ash and told him to choose one of the three Poké Balls on the table. "When I was young, I was a serious Pokémon trainer," the professor explained. "In my old age, I have only three left, but you can have one. Choose!"

Gary was none too pleased. "Hey! Gramps! What about me?" he demanded.

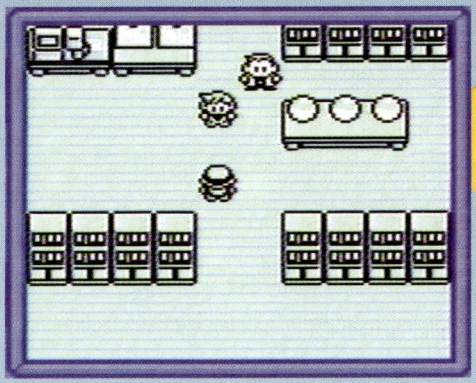

Inside his lab, the Professor offers Ash one of his three Pokémon.

Chapter 1   Ash Meets His First Pokémon

"Be patient, Gary," said the Pokémon Professor. "You can have one, too."

Ash studied the three Poké Balls. It was a tough decision, but finally he selected the Poké Ball on the left. As soon as he picked it up, out popped Charmander—a two-foot-tall, lizard-like Pokémon with a large tail. "So, you want the Fire Pokémon Charmander? This Pokémon is really energetic!" said the Professor.

Ash, grinning from ear to ear, patted Charmander and happily said, "Yes!" He was very excited to finally have his very own Pokémon to train and care for.

Name: Charmander™
Number: 4
Type: Fire

Professor Oak then explained that whenever a Pokémon trainer receives or captures a new Pokémon, he can give it a nickname. Ash decided to call his new Pokémon "Charmer."

The professor next had Gary choose one of the two remaining Poké Balls. Gary quickly selected the middle Poké Ball. It was Squirtle!

Now that both Ash and Gary had their own Pokémon, the professor told them how to take care of them and how to help them grow.

Name: Squirtle™
Number: 7
Type: Water

As Ash turned to leave, Gary called out, "Wait, Ash. Let's check out our Pokémon. Come on, I'll take you on!" Ash jumped at the chance to give Charmer its first challenge.

As any Pokémon trainer can tell you, a Pokémon's strength is rated by its level and number of hit points. When a

Pokémon wins a battle, it earns experience points (Exp). When it obtains enough of these points, its level and strength increase.

Pokémon trainers have to be very careful not to let their Pokémon's hit points get too low while fighting. Every time a Pokémon gets injured, it loses some of its hit points. When a Pokémon loses all of its HP, it faints and can't fight again until its health is restored.

Charmer and Squirtle experience their first Pokémon battle!

Both Charmer and Squirtle were at Level 5. Because Charmer was just starting out, it only knew two moves—Scratch and Growl—and it had only 19 hit points.

After thinking about how best to fight Squirtle, Ash commanded Charmer to use its Scratch attack. In return, Squirtle launched its Tail Whip against Charmer. The two Pokémon traded blows until finally (with just one hit point left!) Charmer hit with another power-packed Scratch—and Gary's new Squirtle fainted! Charmer gained 70 experience points for its victory and was immediately promoted to Level 6. Because Ash had beaten Gary in battle, he was rewarded with ₽175.

Chapter 1   Ash Meets His First Pokémon

"What? Unbelievable! I picked the wrong Pokémon," said a very annoyed Gary. "I'll make my Pokémon fight to toughen it up. Ash and Gramps, smell you later!" Gary ran out of the lab.

Now that Ash had won his first Pokémon contest, he was truly ready to say goodbye to Professor Oak and begin exploring the lands beyond Pallet Town. "Raise your young Pokémon by making it fight," the Professor told Ash as they said goodbye.

 "Raise your young Pokémon by making it fight."

By training Charmer carefully, Ash knew he would make it a champion!

Ash headed back up the path that led to Viridian City. He knew that along the way, he'd be sure to encounter several Wild Pokémon—and so much the better! By beating them in battle, Charmer would become even stronger.

Name:
Pidgey™
Number: 16
Type:
Normal/Flying

All Pokémon trainers know that Wild Pokémon lurk in tall grass. Sure enough, soon after Ash ventured in the grass along the path leading to Viridian City, he ran into his first Wild Pokémon—a Level 3 Pidgey.

Pathways to Adventure

"Go Charmer!" cried Ash, and the battle was joined. Charmer struck first with its Scratch attack. Pidgey, a flying creature, threw out a Gust attack, but Pidgey was clearly no match for Charmer. Charmer quickly defeated the Pidgey and gained 23 more experience points.

His spirits soaring, Ash continued toward Viridian City. He had walked just a little farther when he saw a sign. He stopped to read it: "Route 1—Pallet Town—Viridian City." When Ash looked up, he saw a young man standing near him. "Hi! I work at a Pokémon Mart," the young man said. "It's a convenient shop, so please visit us in Viridian City." Ash learned that this shop sold all sorts of useful things to Pokémon trainers.

To encourage Ash to visit the Mart, the young man gave Ash a free sample: a Potion that could restore some of a Pokémon's hit points. "We also carry Poké Balls for catching Pokémon," added the young man. Poké Balls were just what Ash needed to start his Pokémon collection!

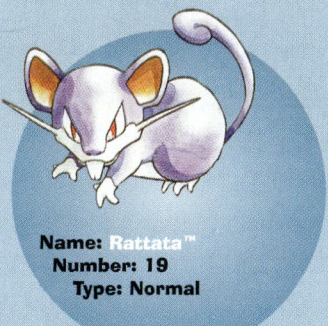

Name: Rattata™
Number: 19
Type: Normal

Ash had just started walking up the winding path to Viridian City when a Level 2 Rattata leaped out of the bushes and startled him.

Ash could have kept Charmer safe by running away from the battle, but Charmer was still in good health and Ash now had a Potion, so he sent his Pokémon into battle once more. Charmer used Scratch again and again until it caused Rattata to faint. Charmer was again victorious! Charmer had gained 24 more experience points—and had advanced to Level 7!

Chapter 1   Ash Meets His First Pokémon

Ash continued on his way. He soon came upon a sign that contained a Pokémon training tip. It read: "The battle moves of Pokémon are limited by their Power Points, PP. To replenish PP, rest your tired Pokémon at a Pokémon Center."

Charmer had already been in four battles. A rest sounded like a great idea.

In any village or city, a Pokémon Center will display a sign that says "Poké" near the front door.

On the outskirts of Viridian City, Ash discovered a building with a sign that said "Poké" in very large letters near the door—a Pokémon Center! Inside, he was greeted warmly by the woman behind the counter. "Welcome to our Pokémon Center," she said. "We heal your Pokémon back to perfect health! Shall we heal your Pokémon?"

Ash handed her the Poké Ball containing Charmer. Within a few seconds, Charmer's HP and PP were completely replenished. "Your Pokémon are fighting fit. We hope to see you again," said the woman with a smile.

Near the Pokémon Center, Ash found a Mart. Remembering his encounter with the young man on the trail, he went in.

Pathways to Adventure

As soon as Ash entered the Mart, the shopkeeper asked if he was from Pallet Town. "Yes," Ash replied, and the shopkeeper handed him a package addressed to Professor Oak. "His order came in. Will you take it to him?" Ash readily agreed to deliver the package. "Say hi to Prof. Oak for me!" the shopkeeper said.

Before leaving, Ash looked around and noticed that the Mart sold Poké Balls, Antidotes, Paralyz Heals, and Burn Heals. Ash knew that Marts in other villages and cities would offer a different selection of items, but when he returned from his errand, he would stock up on Poké Balls here so he could start building his Pokémon collection. For now, he had a job to do.

Ash left the Mart and began to make his way back to Pallet Town.

Jumping over the low hedges, Ash made it back home in no time. First he dropped in on his mom, who suggested he stay for a quick rest. He hadn't realized until then how much he'd done that day. It felt good to nap, but he was quickly rested enough to move on. "You and your Pokémon are looking great!" cried his proud mom. "Take care now."

Not surprisingly, Ash found the professor in the Oak Pokémon Research Lab. "How is my old Pokémon?" asked Professor Oak. "Well, it seems to like you a lot. You must be talented as a Pokémon trainer! What? You have something for me?" he asked, spying the package in Ash's hands. "Ah! This is the custom Poké Ball I ordered," he said as Ash handed him the package. "Thank you!"

Just then, Gary came running into the lab. "Gramps! What did you call me for?"

"Oh right! I have a request of you two," said the professor, looking pointedly at both boys. "On the desk there is my invention, Pokédex! It automatically records data on Pokémon you've seen or caught. It's a high-tech encyclopedia. Ash and Gary, take these with you!

The professor handed one Pokédex to Ash and another to Gary. "To make a complete guide of all the Pokémon in the world, that was my dream," he said sadly. "But, I'm too old! I can't do it! So I want you two to fulfill my dream for me. Get moving you two! This is a great undertaking in Pokémon history!" What an important task Ash had been entrusted with!

"Alright Gramps! Leave it all to me!" Gary crowed. "Ash, I hate to say it, but I don't need you. I know!" he continued, "I'll borrow a Town Map from my sis. I'll tell her not to lend you one! Hahaha!"

With that, Gary ran out of the lab.

"Pokémon around the world wait for you, Ash," said the Professor. As Ash exited the building, he thought to himself, "I gotta catch' em all!"

 "Pokémon around the world wait for you…"

Ash knew he had to leave Pallet Town to build Charmer's strength. But it would be easy for him to get lost out there. He had to get his hands on one of Gary's sister's maps!

Pathways to Adventure

Remembering Gary's threat, Ash was a little concerned as he entered Gary's house and approached his sister, but Ash's quick thinking saved him. "Grandpa asked you to run an errand?" she said. "Here, this will help you!" She handed him his very own map.

Now he could uncover the best routes to follow on his quest! Ash gave it a quick look. The places it showed sounded fantastic—Diglett's Cave! Mt. Moon! Vermilion City! Pokémon Tower! All this and more lay before him. Tucking the map safely away, he headed back toward Viridian City.

His adventure was just beginning....

Chapter 1   Ash Meets His First Pokémon

Ash was anxious to get to Viridian City and stock up on Poké Balls, but he was still up for a few encounters with Wild Pokémon. Charmer had grown so strong now that the Level 3 Rattata that first challenged it along Route 1 fainted in no time. The Level 3 Pidgey that swooped in on Charmer moments later was a little harder to beat, but not much.

Several battles later, Ash reached the entrance to Viridian City. His first stop was the Pokémon Center, where he replenished Charmer's health.

Next he returned to the Poké Mart.

"Hi there! May I help you?" asked the shopkeeper as Ash approached the counter. Ash gathered up six Poké Balls and paid the shopkeeper ₽1200 for them. Ash knew that Marts in other villages and cities sold Great Balls and Ultra Balls, which are more powerful than Poké Balls, but for now the basic Poké Balls sold here would work
just fine.

Ash buys six Poké Balls from the Mart.

After leaving the Mart, Ash explored Viridian City. Near the city's exit, he stumbled upon a gym, which was locked up.

A fellow Pokémon trainer standing outside the building said, "This Pokémon Gym is always closed. I wonder who the leader is?" The building appeared to be vacant.

There weren't any Pokémon trainers looking for a challenge, and every Pokémon trainer knows that Wild Pokémon are never found within cities, so Ash started down the nearby dirt path in hopes of new adventure—and new Pokémon. A wooden sign in the middle of a field read: "Route 2: Viridian City—Pewter City."

Suddenly, a Rattata leaped out at Ash! Charmer quickly trounced the low-level Wild Pokémon. Charmer reached Level 9—and, as a result, learned a new attack called Ember!

Farther down the dirt path, Ash spied a brick building. As he approached this building, he was attacked by another Rattata. Thinking quickly, Ash decided to capture it, but he knew he'd have to move carefully. For Ash to capture the Rattata, Charmer would have to weaken it but not make it faint. Ash cautiously used one of Charmer's Scratch attacks, and the Rattata became weak enough for Ash to throw one of his Poké Balls and capture his first Wild Pokémon!

He then stepped inside the nearby building and ran into a young Pokémon trainer, who remarked, "Rattata may be small, but its bite is wicked! Did you get one?" Further into the building, a female Pokémon trainer warned, "Are you going to Viridian Forest? Be careful, it's a natural maze!"

After taking the warning in, Ash noticed a door on the opposite side of the room. He walked through it and found himself at the edge of Viridian Forest.

Chapter 2 Ash Expands His Pokémon Collection

A Pokémon trainer was hanging out near a large tree. When Ash walked up to greet him, the trainer said, "I came here with some friends. They're out for Pokémon fights." Ash was sure to meet up with them, which meant more training fights for Charmer!

⭐ **"Are you going to Viridian Forest? Be careful, it's a natural maze!"**

Ash hadn't gone far into the forest when he spotted a wild Caterpie. Instead of making this Wild Pokémon faint, Ash decided to catch it and add it to his collection. He commanded Charmer to weaken the bug-like Pokémon with one Scratch. As soon as the Caterpie was caught by the Poké Ball, information about it instantly appeared in Ash's Pokédex.

Name: Caterpie™
Number: 10
Type: Bug

Ash continued to search the forest. Along the way, he found a Poké Ball that another Pokémon trainer had dropped.

A little farther into the dense forest, Ash noticed a Pokémon trainer walking toward him. He was carrying a large net. "Yo, you can't jam out if you're a Pokémon trainer," said the young man, who called himself Bug Catcher.

Bug Catcher then challenged Ash to a Pokémon battle. Before Ash could respond, Bug Catcher reached into his

Pathways to Adventure

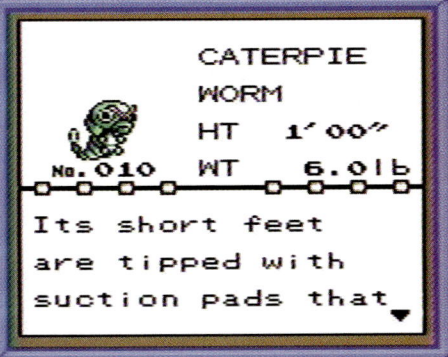

Each time Ash captures a new Pokémon, information about it automatically appears on his Pokédex screen.

sack and tossed out a Poké Ball containing a Level 7 Weedle.

Of Ash's three Pokémon, Charmer was the strongest. Quick as a wink, Ash commanded Charmer to use its new Ember attack to weaken Bug Catcher's Weedle. This attack turned out to be so powerful, Weedle immediately fainted!

But the battle wasn't over yet; the rival trainer brought out a second Poké Ball. A Level 7 Kakuna burst out and went for Charmer. Again, Charmer attacked with Ember. Kakuna was visibly weakened, but gathered itself up and threw out its Defense move; Charmer answered with a Scratch. The battle raged on. When it was over, Charmer was raised to Level 10!

Name: Weedle™
Number: 13
Type: Bug/Poison

Name: Kakuna™
Number: 14
Type: Bug/Poison

Not willing to give up, Bug Catcher ordered his final Pokémon, another Level 7 Weedle, to attack. This Weedle

Chapter 2 Ash Expands His Pokémon Collection

tried Poison Stings and String Shots against Charmer, but luckily these attacks had little impact. After four Scratch attacks, Weedle fainted, and Bug Catcher admitted his defeat. "Huh? I ran out of Pokémon!" cried Bug Catcher, a bit shocked that he had lost three battles in a row.

The victorious Ash left Bug Catcher and wandered deeper into the forest. As he traveled, he found an Antidote and Potion lying on the ground and happily picked them up. Not long after, Ash met up with Bug Catcher again. The two Pokémon trainers engaged in battle, but Bug Catcher's new Pokémon were quickly defeated. Ash left him and continued his search for Wild Pokémon.

It wasn't long before Ash encountered a wild Level 5 Metapod. He knew just what to do: Charmer's first Scratch weakened the Metapod enough for Ash to catch it with a Poké Ball. Ash excitedly counted the four Pokémon in his collection; he was off to a great start—Professor Oak would be so proud of him!

Name:
Metapod™
Number: 11
Type: Bug

Ash was just about to set off again, when from out of the bushes jumped a wild Level 5 Pikachu!

Name:
Pikachu™
Number: 25
Type: Electric

To boost his Caterpie's experience points, Ash first had it send out a Tackle, closely followed by a String Shot. Pikachu was unfazed, so Ash brought out Charmer to weaken the creature. Ash realized, to his dismay, that switching

Pathways to Adventure

Pokémon mid-battle allowed his opponent to attack first, which could put him at a disadvantage.

Pikachu's Thundershock was very powerful, but it was no match for Charmer's Scratch. After two Scratch attacks from Charmer, the wild Pikachu was about ready to pass out. Ash threw a Poké Ball at the Wild Pokémon and managed to catch it just before it fainted.

Ash encounters his first wild Pikachu!

Ash had captured his very own Pikachu! According to the Pokédex, a Pikachu is 1 foot, 4 inches high, weighs 13 pounds, and uses electricity to launch its attacks. Ash nicknamed his new Pikachu "Pikoo." To his delight, Ash discovered that his newest Pokémon was already capable of using a Thundershock attack *and* a Growl attack.

Although all of Ash's Pokémon were weak from battles, Charmer still had enough HP to take on the additional Wild Pokémon Ash encountered as he walked toward Pewter City. Soon he would need to visit a Pokémon Center to replenish all his Pokémon.

Chapter 2   Ash Expands His Pokémon Collection

Ash discovered Charmer could make many lower-ranking Wild Pokémon faint with just one attack. But when he wanted to *catch* a Wild Pokémon, he realized it was better to use one of his lower-level Pokémon to just weaken the Wild Pokémon.

As Ash neared the edge of the forest, he saw Bug Catcher waiting for him. Ash really wanted to get to Pewter City, but Bug Catcher would have none of it. "Hey, wait up! What's the hurry?" asked Bug Catcher, who released a Level 9 Weedle without even so much as an invitation to battle. All it took was one of Charmer's extremely hot Ember attacks to make Bug Catcher's Weedle faint. Charmer moved right on up to Level 13. "I give! You're good at this!" sighed Bug Catcher.

After saying farewell to Bug Catcher, Ash came across a sign that said: "Leaving Viridian Forest. Pewter City Ahead." Just past the sign, Ash entered an unlocked building and bumped into two strangers.

"Have you noticed the bushes on the roadside? They can be cut down by a special Pokémon move," explained one of the strangers. Ash knew this move was made possible by something called a Hidden Machine 01 (HM01). Once Ash obtained an HM01, he'd be able to teach one or more of his Pokémon the Cut maneuver, which could be used in battle or used to destroy certain obstacles in his path—like bushes.

The second stranger encouraged Ash to search everywhere for different types of Pokémon. After chatting with this stranger, Ash noticed a door on the opposite side of the room. This door turned out to be the entrance to the second leg of Route 2, which, according to Ash's map, went toward Pewter City. Luckily for Ash's tired-out Pokémon, he didn't

encounter any Wild Pokémon or Pokémon trainers along this part of Route 2.

Once in Pewter City, Ash went directly to the Pokémon Center to heal all his Pokémon.

"Welcome to our Pokémon Center. We heal your Pokémon back to perfect health!" promised the woman behind the counter. Ash gladly handed over his Poké Balls. In his collection thus far was Charmer, along with Metapod, Caterpie, Rattata, and Pikoo the Pikachu.

Now that his Pokémon were once again fighting fit, Ash decided to explore Pewter City. He knew somewhere in this city there was a Gym where Brock, one of the world-famous Pokémon Leaders, could be found. If Ash's Pokémon could beat Brock's Pokémon, Ash would be awarded the official Pokémon League Boulderbadge. Fighting Brock would be very difficult; everyone knew that Brock had a well-trained Level 12 Geodude and a Level 14 Onix, more powerful than any Pokémon Ash had yet encountered!

Name: Geodude™
Number: 74
Type: Rock/Ground

Name: Onix™
Number: 95
Type: Rock/Ground

Ash had to have that Boulderbadge! To successfully defeat Brock, he would first have to boost the strength of his Pokémon by fighting more lower-level Pokémon. He'd also need to drop into the Pewter City Mart and stock up on some useful items. Ash walked quickly through the city; he had a mission to accomplish!

Chapter 2   Ash Expands His Pokémon Collection

CHAPTER 3

Ash Visits the Pewter City Gym

After visiting the Mart in Pewter City, Ash immediately made for the city's Gym. Ash knew Brock and several other Pokémon trainers were waiting inside the Gym to challenge him.

Ash prepares to face his first Pokémon Leader inside Pewter City's Gym.

Just inside the Gym's entrance, Ash ran into a young man wearing glasses, who was hanging out in the large lobby. "Hiya! I can tell you have what it takes to become a Pokémon champ!" the stranger complimented him. "I'm no trainer, but I can tell you how to win," he added.

Ash readily agreed to listen to the stranger's tips. The young man continued, "The first Pokémon out in a match is at the top of the Pokémon List! By changing the order of Pokémon, matches could be made easier."

Ash checked his own Pokémon List; Charmer, his strongest Pokémon, was listed first. That meant it would be the first to fight whenever Ash was challenged. Ash decided not to change the order just yet.

Storming into the lobby, a tough Pokémon trainer named Jr. Trainer shouted out to Ash. "Stop right there, kid!" he yelled. "You're still light years from facing Brock!"

Pathways to Adventure

Jr. Trainer then released a Level 11 Diglett. One of Charmer's Ember attacks cut Diglett's HP in half, but Diglett still had plenty of strength to Scratch Charmer up pretty badly. Finally, Charmer finished off its opponent with its own Scratch attack.

Charmer had gained 190 Experience Points, but the battle wasn't over yet! Without missing a beat, Jr. Trainer sent out a Level 11 Sandshrew in hopes of defeating Ash. Sandshrew's Scratch attacks were just as nasty as Diglett's. To heal some of Charmer's wounds so it wouldn't faint, Ash grabbed a Potion from his inventory and used it on his Pokémon. Charmer then launched an Ember attack and seared its opponent. The fight was long and intense, but Sandshrew finally gave in to Charmer's constant barrage of Ember and Scratch attacks. Ash was pleased to see Charmer boosted to Level 14.

Name: Diglett™
Number: 50
Type: Ground

Name: Sandshrew™
Number: 27
Type: Ground

"Darn! Light years isn't time! It measures distance!" exclaimed Jr. Trainer after Ash defeated him. Jr. Trainer had mistakenly said Ash needed trillions of *miles* of experience before facing Brock rather than trillions of *years*—and Ash had proven him wrong. Jr. Trainer then stepped aside and allowed Ash to walk into the heart of the Gym, where Brock was waiting for him.

Chapter **3**   Ash Visits the Pewter City Gym

"I'm Brock! I'm Pewter's Gym Leader! I believe in rock hard defense and determination. That's why my Pokémon are all the rock-type. Do you still want to challenge me?" asked Brock. Ash accepted the challenge without hesitation. "Fine then! Show me your best!" cried Brock as he tossed out a Level 12 Geodude to kick off the battle.

Ash challenges Brock—a Pokémon Leader.

Charmer gave all it had, but its Ember attack wasn't too effective at first. Geodude's first Tackle weakened Charmer so much, Ash was forced to use another Potion to keep his Pokémon going. It ultimately took five Ember attacks and two Potions for Charmer to defeat Brock's Geodude.

 "I believe in rock hard defense and determination!"

Instead of being allowed a much-needed rest, Charmer was immediately forced to confront Brock's Level 14 Onix. This snake-like creature looked like it was made out of rock, and its face was large and mean. Onix's Tackle and Bide attacks were powerful, so Ash kept a constant eye on Charmer's HP as the two Pokémon traded blows. But Charmer's repeated Ember attacks seemed to be doing the trick.

Just when Charmer appeared to be winning, Onix launched an Energy attack. Charmer's HP drained to zero! This turn of events took Ash by complete surprise. With Charmer temporarily out of the fight, Ash called upon his Level 3 Rattata to finish off the greatly-weakened Onix with Tackle. It took five Tackle attacks, but Rattata was finally able to make Onix faint.

Rattata grew to Level 7 and received a new skill, Quick Attack, as a reward. Ash had successfully defeated Brock!

"I took you for granted," Brock admitted. "As proof of your victory, here's the Boulderbadge." Brock handed Ash this special medallion and said, "That's an official Pokémon League Badge. Its bearer's Pokémon become more powerful!"

Beating Brock was Ash's first big step toward becoming a Pokémon Master. In addition to receiving the special Boulderbadge, he earned ₽ 1386 and was given something called a Technical Machine (TM) 34 by Brock. Ash used TM34 to teach Pikoo, his Pikachu, the Bide fighting move. Ash was delighted to discover that Bide allows a Pokémon to absorb damage in battle and then pay it back double!

Ash learned that he could use each of the 50 different TMs, as he got them, to teach his Pokémon a new skill or attack

move, but some TMs only work with certain types of Pokémon. Because each Pokémon can only master four skills or attack moves at one time, Ash, as a responsible Pokémon trainer, would need to decide which TMs are best to use on which Pokémon. He also learned that Hidden Machines (HMs) work just like TMs except that they can be used as many times as a trainer wants and taught to many different Pokémon.

As Ash left the gym, Brock encouraged him, "There are all kinds of trainers in the world. You appear to be very gifted as a Pokémon trainer! Go to the Gym in Cerulean and test your abilities!"

Ash said goodbye to Brock and planned his route to Cerulean. Ash would have to travel along Route 3 to Mt. Moon and then take Route 4. Of course, Ash was sure to encounter many types of Wild Pokémon, so before leaving Pewter City, he returned to the Mart and increased his inventory so it now included 5 Potions, 1 Antidote, 8 Poké Balls, and the Town Map.

A quick stop at the Pokémon Center was also necessary to replenish the health of his battle-weary Pokémon. Before leaving Pewter City, Ash decided to drop into the city's most popular tourist attraction, The Museum of Science.

He paid his ₽ 50 admission and explored the museum's two floors. Inside the museum, he added data about two extinct Pokémon, Aerodactyl and Kabutops, to his Pokédex; it was information that Professor Oak would find extremely interesting.

Name: Aerodactyl™
Number: 142
Type: Rock/Flying

Pathways to Adventure

Leaving the museum, Ash noticed a building next door, but the path was blocked by several bushes. To get past this obstacle, Ash realized he'd need to get his hands on a HM01 and teach his Pokémon the Cut maneuver. There wasn't much he could do about it now, so Ash made a note to return and explore the strange building later.

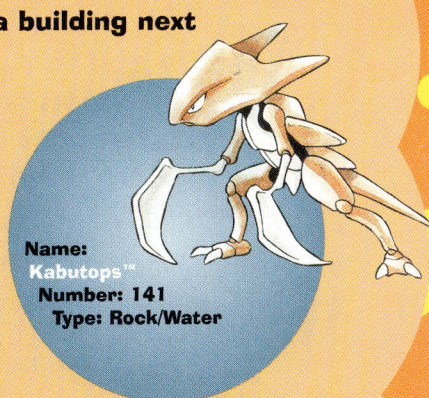

Name: Kabutops™
Number: 141
Type: Rock/Water

Ash headed toward Route 3. Near the route's entrance, he saw a sign that said, "Notice! Thieves have been stealing Pokémon fossils at Mt. Moon! Please call Pewter Police with any info."

Along Route 3, Ash met up with more than ten different Pokémon trainers, all of whom challenged him to battles. These fights gave Ash a chance to help all his Pokémon gain experience points. Most of the trainers in this area had Pidgey, Spearow, and Jigglypuff Pokémon in their collections, but all of the Pokémon were relatively weak.

Name: Spearow™
Number: 21
Type: Normal/Flying

Early in their Route 3 journey, Charmer's Level grew to 15, and it automatically learned to perform the Leer fighting move, which temporarily decreases an opponent's defenses. Before Ash left Route 3, Charmer had reached Level 16 and evolved from a Charmander into a Charmeleon!

Chapter 3 Ash Visits the Pewter City Gym

As Ash walked past a sign that said "Route 3—Mt. Moon Ahead," he noticed a young trainer trying to catch his breath. "Whew... I better take a rest. That tunnel from Cerulean takes a lot out of you," wheezed the stranger. Just then, Ash noticed a Pokémon Center located near the entrance to Mt. Moon.

Name:
Jigglypuff™
Number: 39
Type: Normal

Once inside the Pokémon Center, the woman behind the counter healed Ash's Pokémon, and Ash started thinking about the many legends he had heard about Mt. Moon.

The mountain was rumored to have two floors and a basement, all filled with tunnels and secret passageways. It was a maze that was very easy to get lost in. Because it was so dark, Pokémon trainers often dropped useful items without realizing it.

Name:
Charmeleon™
Number: 5
Type: Fire

Getting lost inside Mt. Moon was certainly a possibility. If this happened, Ash could use an Escape Rope—if he could find one! This rope would transport him out of the area and back to the entrance, where he was right now.

Gathering up his courage, Ash began his exploration of Mt. Moon.

POKéMON

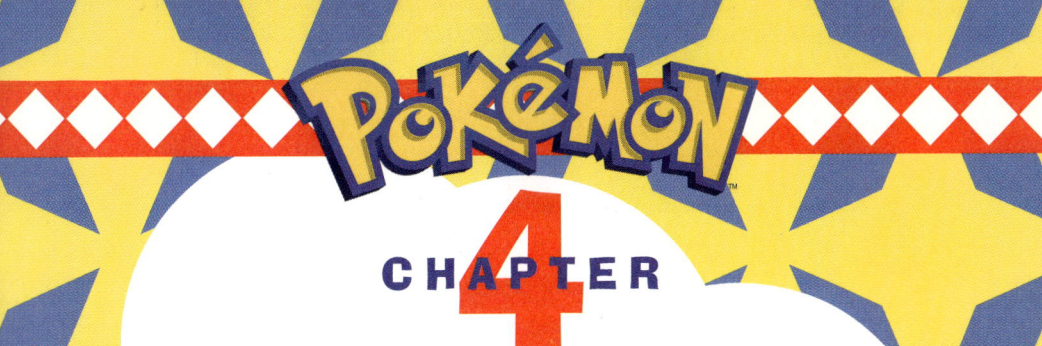

CHAPTER 4

The Journey to Cerulean City and Beyond

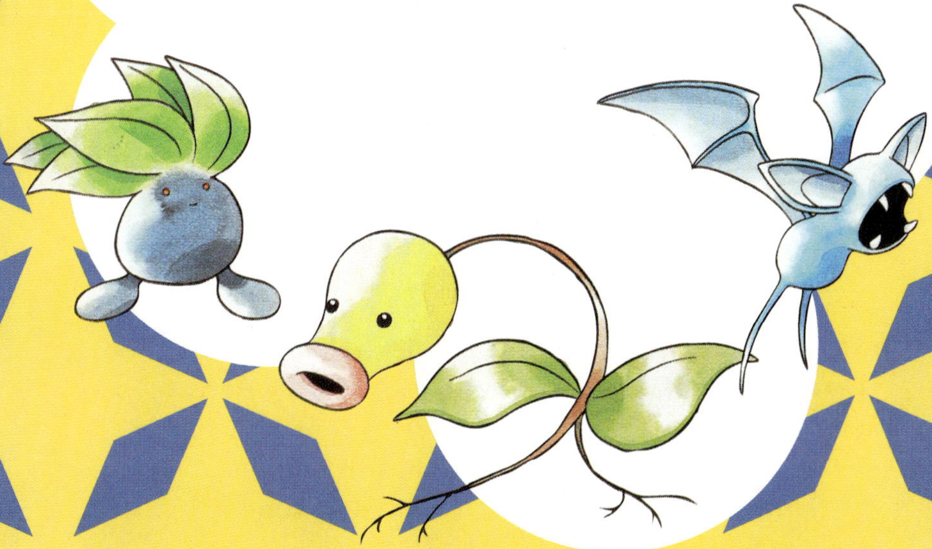

As soon as Ash entered the forbidding Mt. Moon, he found himself in a large cavern. He was greeted by a Level 6 Zubat flying wildly overhead. Using Pikoo's Thundershock, the Zubat was quickly weakened, allowing Ash to add this Pokémon to his collection. Walking forward, Ash read a wooden sign that warned, "Beware! Zubat is a blood sucker!"

A young trainer named Lass was standing next to this sign, waiting for her friends. She challenged Ash using her Level 14 Clefairy, but Charmer's Scratch and Ember attacks defeated Lass's Pokémon easily enough.

Name: Zubat™
Number: 41
Type: Poison/Flying

With another victory under his belt, Ash set out to explore Mt. Moon. After traveling down the first stairwell in the dark caves, Ash followed the underground passageway to the next staircase. He soon found himself on the second basement level. A member of Team Rocket, wearing the black Team uniform, was stationed in the corner.

Name: Clefairy™
Number: 35
Type: Normal

Ash knew all about Team Rocket; it was an organization of gangsters who used their Pokémon for evil. Team Rocket's goal was to conquer the world!

The gangster challenged Ash to a battle by tossing out a Level 11 Sandshrew, followed by a Level 11 Rattata, and then a Level 11 Zubat. Ash had several of his weaker Pokémon launch one attack each, and then used Charmer to finish off each of the evil trainer's Pokémon.

The Team Rocket trainer was not accustomed to losing. "I blew it!" yelled the gangster. Ash, on the other hand, watched his Caterpie evolve into a Level 7 Metapod!

Continuing on his way, Ash found one HP Up, which he used on his Pikachu to boost its HP meter by one point. Without warning, a wild Level 9 Geodude appeared. Ash wanted to add this rock-type Pokémon to his collection, so he weakened it using three of Charmer's Scratch attacks before tossing an empty Poké Ball at the creature.

Retracing his steps, Ash returned to the staircase that he had taken from the first floor of Mt. Moon. He began searching for the next staircase he would need to follow. Along the way, he encountered many Wild Pokémon, and he once again ran into Lass.

"Wow! It's way bigger in here than I thought!" marveled Lass. She was excited because she had caught several new Pokémon and was anxious to test them in battle. She challenged Ash using a Level 11 Oddish and a Level 11 Bellsprout. Charmer, now a Level 19, was easily able to beat Lass's new Pokémon using one Ember attack on Oddish and two Scratch attacks on Bellsprout.

Name: Oddish™
Number: 43
Type: Grass/Poison

Leaving Lass and venturing deep into the heart of Mt. Moon, Ash found the next staircase he was looking for. It wasn't long before he encountered another member of Team Rocket standing near what looked like a Poké Ball lying on the ground. "We're pulling a big job here! Get lost, kid!" shouted the Team Rocket member, who wasn't happy at Ash's intrusion.

Chapter 4   The Journey to Cerulean City and Beyond

Name:
Bellsprout™
Number: 69
Type: Grass/Poison

"Go Charmer!" cried Ash, fending off the gangster's Level 12 Ekans with some difficulty. Finally, the snake-like Ekans out of the way, Ash was able to grab the Poké Ball from the ground. It turned out to be a TM01, which Ash used to teach Pikoo the Mega Punch attack. Because Pokémon can only master four fighting moves at a time, Ash decided that his Pikachu had to forget the Growl attack so it could learn the more powerful Mega Punch.

Hidden near a large rock in the same cavern, Ash found an Ether on the ground. Ash could use Ether to add 10 PP to one of his Pokémon's attack moves or special abilities. A few minutes later, near another staircase, Ash came across a Moon Stone lying on the ground. He grabbed it; a Pokéman trainer could use a Moon Stone to cause some types of Pokémon to instantly evolve!

Name:
Ekans™
Number: 23
Type: Poison

After capturing a wild Paras, Ash continued his quest through the maze-like caves. Climbing back up the ladder to the first floor of Mt. Moon, Ash ran into a trainer known as Youngster, who threw out three Pokémon in rapid succession—to no avail. "Losing stinks!" exclaimed Youngster in disgust.

Within sight of the next staircase, Ash encountered a rather large man, named Hiker, who tested his two Level 10 Geodudes and Level 10 Onix against Ash.

After beating Hiker, Charmer reached Level 21. A little closer to the staircase, Ash noticed a wild Clefairy, which

he decided to weaken using his Geodude's Tackle attack before adding it to his collection.

With the Clefairy now in his collection, Ash grabbed the nearby Moon Stone and scrambled down the staircase. A tunnel led him to another staircase, which deposited him in the second basement.

Name: Paras™
Number: 46
Type: Bug/Grass

Here, Ash encountered another member of Team Rocket, who appeared to be guarding the area. "Little kids should leave grown-ups alone!" taunted the gangster before tossing out his only Pokémon, a Level 16 Raticate. Once Ash's Pokémon beat the Raticate, he was allowed to pass.

Ash followed the pathway, now making a point to conserve his Pokémon's energy by running away from Wild Pokémon attacks. To get past the remaining Team Rocket members hiding out in Mt. Moon, Ash knew he'd need his Pokémon to be strong.

Name: Raticate™
Number: 20
Type: Normal

Ash soon spotted another Team Rocket member; this one was loitering near an opening that Ash needed to pass through. The gangster told him, "Team Rocket will find the fossils, then revive and sell them for cash!"

So that was what Team Rocket was up to! Ash knew he'd have to do whatever he could to stop them. For starters, he could defeat the Team Rocket member who had revealed his organization's diabolical plans.

Chapter 4 The Journey to Cerulean City and Beyond

Without further ado, the gangster grabbed one of his Poké Balls, which opened to reveal a Level 13 Rattata. Ash swiftly commanded Charmer to use Ember—but Charmer's Ember attack was out of PP! Not wanting to take any chances, Ash reached into his Items inventory and used the Ether to replenish some of Charmer's Ember. After a lengthy battle in which Ash used all of his Pokémon, he managed to beat this Team Rocket member. He was immediately greeted by yet another member of the criminal group, who was standing right next to two Pokémon fossils.

 "Team Rocket will find the fossils, then revive and sell them for cash!"

"Hey, stop!" shouted the gangster, whose name was Super Nerd. "I found these fossils. They're both mine!"

Ash wasn't about to let Team Rocket steal these ancient Pokémon fossils! Super Nerd's Level 12 Grimer launched its initial attack, and Ash called on Charmer. A mega battle ensued. Both trainers were evenly matched, but thanks to some fancy Pokémon switching, Ash managed to keep his Pokémon strong, while weakening all of Super Nerd's Pokémon!

"Okay! I'll share," decided Super Nerd. "We'll each take one." Ash knew he didn't have a choice, so he reluctantly agreed to take only one of the fossils. He grabbed the Dome Fossil and made a mad dash for the exit.

After taking the nearby staircase, Ash found himself bathed in sunlight. He breathed a sigh of relief. By exploring Mt. Moon carefully, Ash had found two Potions, Rare Candy, Escape Rope, two Moon Stones, a TM01, an HP Up, and a TM 12, which gave him the ability to teach certain types of Pokemon the Water Gun attack.

Name:
Grimer™
Number: 88
Type: Poison

Just ahead was a wooden sign that read, "Route 4: Mt. Moon—Cerulean City." Ash followed the path exactly, being careful to avoid possible detours along the way.

The trip along Route 4 was a very short one. Along this path, Ash found a Poké Ball containing a TM04, which gave him the ability to teach one of his Pokémon the Whirlwind attack. He decided to save this TM and use it later. Right now, he just wanted to reach Cerulean City.

In no time, Ash found himself at the entrance to the city. He went straight to the Pokémon Center, which was located near the Trading Post, to heal his Pokémon.

He then examined the Pokémon in his collection. He was currently carrying: Charmer (Level 22), Pikoo (Level 6), Metapod (Level 6), Geodude (Level 9), Rattata (Level 5), and Caterpie (Level 4). From his Pokédex, Ash found that he had already encountered 26 different species of Pokémon and had nine in his collection. Ash strolled over to the computer in the corner of the Pokémon Center and explored it a little; he could store inventory items, check out his Pokémon, and use something called Someone's PC. Curious!

Chapter 4 The Journey to Cerulean City and Beyond

His business at the Center done, Ash strolled around Cerulean City. He discovered a Bike Shop, but couldn't afford the incredibly high price of a bicycle. Undaunted, Ash dropped into the Mart and purchased five Potions, five Poké Balls, two Antidotes, one Awakening, two Repels, and a Paralyz Heal. Ash was careful to keep some money in his pocket in case he needed it for an emergency.

There wasn't a whole lot to do in Cerulean City, so Ash took his empty Poké Balls and headed to the tall grassy areas at the end of Route 4 in search of Wild Pokémon. Here he came across a Level 6 Sandshrew and used Pikoo's Mega Punch to weaken and catch it. In the same area, Ash found a wild Level 10 Spearow, which he also added to his collection.

Ash then returned to Cerulean City and headed to the Gym in search of some action. After all, Brock had told him to find the Cerulean City Gym Leader, Misty, and challenge her. Inside the Gym, which resembled a swimming pool, Ash was greeted by a trainer known as Swimmer. He soon learned that in this Gym, the trainers specialized in water-type Pokémon. Swimmer challenged Ash by releasing one of her Level 16 Horsea Pokémon, followed closely by a Level 16 Shellder. Charmer's Scratch attacks proved particularly useful against these types of Pokémon.

After Swimmer's defeat, one of Misty's other students, Jr. Trainer, challenged Ash. "I'm more than good enough for you!" she cried as she hauled out a Level 19 Goldeen.

Once Ash had defeated Jr. Trainer, his skills caught Misty's attention. "Hi, you

Name: Horsea™
Number: 116
Type: Water

are a new face," she said. "Trainers who want to turn pro have to have a policy about Pokémon! What is your approach when you fight Pokémon? My policy is an all-out offensive with water-type Pokémon!"

Name: Shellder™
Number: 90
Type: Water

Realizing that he wasn't yet ready to face Misty's powerful Pokémon, Ash decided to temporarily leave Cerulean City and check out Route 24. Ash found his old rival, Gary, standing near the bridge to Route 24.

"Yo! You're still struggling along back here? I'm doing great! I caught a bunch of strong and smart Pokémon! Here, let me see what you caught, Ash," said Gary, who challenged Ash with a Level 18 Pidgeotto, followed by a Level 15 Abra, a Level 15 Ratatta, and finally a Level 17 Squirtle.

Name: Goldeen™
Number: 118
Type: Water

Ash responded to these challenges using Charmer, his most powerful Pokémon. Gary finally shrieked, "Hey! Take it easy! You won already! Hey, guess what?" Gary added, "I went to Bill's and got him to show me his rare Pokémon! That added a lot of pages to my Pokédex! After all, Bill's world famous as a Pokémaniac! He invented the Pokémon

"Hey! Take it easy! You won already!"

Chapter 4 The Journey to Cerulean City and Beyond

Storage System on PC! Since you're using his system, go thank him! Well, I better get rolling! Smell ya later!" So that's what Someone's PC, on the Pokémon Center computer, was about!

Name: Pidgeotto™
Number: 17
Type: Normal/Flying

It turned out that Bill lived in the Sea Cottage at the end of Route 25. Gary ran off toward Cerulean City, while Ash headed in the opposite direction, across the nearby bridge. On the bridge, Ash encountered five Pokémon trainers, all of whom, of course, challenged him.

Name: Abra™
Number: 63
Type: Psychic

"This is Nugget Bridge. Beat us 5 trainers and win a fabulous prize! Think you got what it takes?" asked Bug Catcher, his first opponent.

By the time Ash reached the second trainer on the bridge, Charmer had reached Level 24 and had learned the Rage attack, which would allow Charmer's

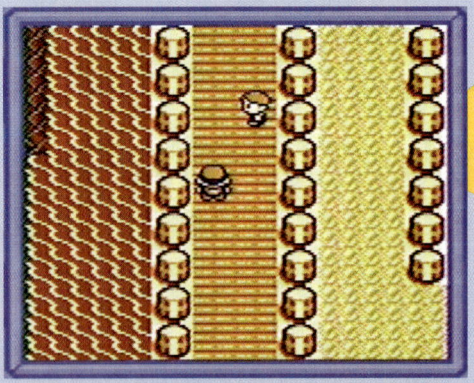

To cross this bridge on Route 24, Ash needs to defeat five Pokémon trainers.

Pathways to Adventure

attack to get stronger as it received damage from an oncoming attack. Before continuing to fight, Ash decided to replace Charmer's Growl with Rage.

Despite Ash's strong Pokémon, the fights on the bridge were grueling. But Ash managed to defeat all five trainers! His fabulous prize was a Nugget, which Ash could sell at a Mart for ₽ 5000! The trainer who gave Ash his prize turned out to be a member of Team Rocket in disguise. "Congratulations! You beat our 5 contest trainers! You just earned a fabulous prize! By the way, would you like to join Team Rocket? We're a group dedicated to evil using Pokémon! Want to join?" Ash didn't have to think twice before refusing the offer.

"I'm telling you to join!" exclaimed the Team Rocket member, quickly losing his patience. "Okay, you need convincing! I'll make you an offer you can't refuse!" The gangster challenged Ash with his Level 15 Ekans and Level 15 Zubat. After a rather short battle, Ash was victorious. "With your ability, you could become a top leader in Team Rocket," said the defeated gangster, who was forced to allow Ash to pass by.

Near the end of the bridge, Ash found a TM45, which would allow him to teach certain types of Pokémon how to launch Thunder Wave attacks.

Ash stepped off the bridge and onto Route 25, heading toward Sea Cottage. Along this route, Pokémon trainers challenged him to seemingly-nonstop battles. Ash welcomed the chance to help all his Pokémon gain experience points—and his Metapod soon evolved into a Level 11

Chapter 4   The Journey to Cerulean City and Beyond

Butterfree!

Ash finally arrived at Bill's Sea Cottage, which was furnished with several very large, high-tech machines with flashing lights. A Pokémon crawled up to Ash and said, "Hiya. I'm a Pokémon. No I'm not! Call me Bill. I'm a true blue Pokémaniac. Hey, what's with that skeptical look?" protested Bill. "I'm not joshing you. I screwed up an experiment and got combined with a Pokémon! So, how about it? Help me out here!"

Name: Butterfree™
Number: 12
Type: Bug/Flying

Ash was more than happy to help the adventurous Bill transform back into a person. "When I'm in the Teleporter, go to my PC and run the Cell Separation System," Bill instructed him.

Bill's Sea Cottage has some very interesting machinery at work.

Ash walked over to the computer while Bill enclosed himself in the Teleporter. As Ash initiated the Cell Separator, he heard a loud hum and then a hiss. A moment later, Bill,

Pathways to Adventure

a person again, stepped out of the Teleporter and thanked Ash for his help.

"Yeehaw! Thanks, bud! I owe you one!" said Bill. "Oh here, maybe this'll do." He handed Ash a ticket for the S.S. Anne. "That cruise ship, S.S. Anne, is in Vermilion City. Its passengers are all trainers! They invited me to their party, but I can't stand fancy do's. Why don't you go instead of me?"

A high seas cruise! Looking at his Town Map, Ash decided that the best way to reach Vermilion City was to go back to Cerulean City. Ash backtracked to Cerulean City and first stopped at the Pokémon Center to heal his Pokémon.

On his way out of Cerulean City, Ash noticed a police officer standing outside a house. After hearing that the house had been robbed by a Team Rocket member, Ash decided to investigate. He searched the house for clues and then left by the back door. In the backyard, Ash was attacked by a disguised member of Team Rocket.

Ash fought off the Team Rocket member's Pokémon and retrieved the TM28 that the gangster had stolen. The TM28 could give certain types of Pokemon the ability to Dig. Continuing along Route 5, Ash found a small building, which turned out to be the entrance to an underground path that connected Route 5 to Route 6! Ash soon reached Vermilion City, located near the ocean.

Ash's first stop was the Pokémon Center; he then took a walk around the city before heading to the cruise ship. His trip aboard the S.S. Anne was sure to be an exciting one!

Chapter 4 The Journey to Cerulean City and Beyond

Pokémon

The citizens of Vermilion City were excited about the Pokémon bash about to take place aboard the S.S. Anne. Some of the people Ash met even wanted to trade Pokémon in preparation for the party.

Ash dropped into the Pokémon Fan Club and ran into the club's president. "I have collected over 100 Pokémon. I'm very fussy when it comes to Pokémon! Did you come visit to hear about my Pokémon?" asked the club's leader. Ash, of course, listened intently.

After telling Ash all about his Rapidash and other Pokémon, the Club president realized how much of Ash's time he had taken up. "Oops! Look at the time! I kept you too long!" he cried. "Thanks for hearing me out! I want you to have this!" He handed Ash a Bike Voucher for a free bicycle from the Bike Shop back in Cerulean City. "I hope you like cycling!" said the club's president as he sent Ash on his way.

Name:
Rapidash™
Number: 78
Type: Fire

In the building to the left of the city's Pokémon Center, Ash met a trainer who was known as the Fishing Guru. "I simply looove fishing! Do you like to fish?" he asked. Ash replied, "Yes," and was rewarded with a special gift. "Take this and fish, young one!" said the Fishing Guru and handed Ash an Old Rod for catching Wild Pokémon from the water.

Ash then set out for Vermilion Harbor and the S.S. Anne. On the way, he passed the city's Gym, but its pathway was blocked.

Directly in front of the S.S. Anne, a sailor was collecting tickets from Pokémon trainers as they boarded the ship.

Pathways to Adventure

Ash flashed the ticket that Bill had given him and went aboard. First he explored some cabins and collected several items, including a TM08, an Ether, a Max Potion, a TM44, a Great Ball, a Max Ether, and a Rare Candy.

Ash flashes his ticket at the sailor to get aboard the S.S. Anne, a giant luxury cruise ship.

On the second floor of the ship, Ash once again ran into Gary. "Bonjour Ash! Imagine seeing you here!" Gary exclaimed. "Ash, were you really invited? So how's your Pokédex coming? I already caught 40 kinds, pal! Different kinds are everywhere! Crawl around in grassy areas!" he hinted and threw four different Pokémon at Ash, challenging him once again to battle.

"Different kinds are everywhere! Crawl around in grassy areas!"

Ash's Pokémon defeated Gary's Level 19 Pidgeotto, Level 16 Raticate, Level 18 Kadabra, and Level 20 Wartortle, but

Gary gave Ash some useful advice anyway. "I heard there was a Cut master on board. But, he was just a seasick old man! Cut itself is really useful! You should go see him! Smell ya!" With that, Gary ran off. Ash decided to search for the old man down the nearby staircase.

The Captain's quarters were at the bottom of the staircase; Ash entered without hesitation. It turned out that the Captain of the S.S. Anne was the Cut master Gary had mentioned, and indeed he was very sick. "Ooargh. I feel hideous. Urrp! Seasick," cried the Captain. Ash sympathetically rubbed the Captain's back.

"Whew! Thank you! I feel much better!" said the Captain gratefully. "You want to see my Cut technique? I could show you if I wasn't ill. I know! You can have this! Teach it to your Pokémon and you can see it Cut any time." The Captain handed Ash HM01, which Ash immediately used to teach Charmer the Cut technique!

He then decided it was more important to continue his quest for new Pokémon than it was to attend the S.S. Anne's party, so Ash left the ship and returned to Vermilion City.

Ash discovered that before battling a Gym Leader, he first had to beat a Pokémon Leader at another Gym. He suddenly remembered Misty, the Pokémon Leader from Cerulean City. Maybe his Pokémon were strong enough to defeat her now!

Retracing his steps, Ash set off for Cerulean City. Along the way, he made a point of walking through the tall grassy areas to catch Wild Pokémon, like the Level 15 Bellsprout he found near Vermilion City.

At Cerulean City, his first stop was the Pokémon Center. Ash next returned to the Bike Shop and exchanged the Bike Voucher for a shiny new bicycle!

Ash trades in his Bike Voucher for a shiny new bicycle at the Bike Shop in Cerulean City.

It was now time to return to the Gym and challenge Misty. Her two water-based Pokémon, a Level 18 Staryu and a Level 21 Starmie, would be very difficult to defeat. After greeting Misty, Ash began the battle by sending out his low-level Pokémon to weaken Misty's Pokémon. He then had Charmer inflict as much damage as it could on Staryu and Starmie.

Winning this battle earned Ash Misty's Cascadebadge, his second official Pokémon Trainer's Badge. "Wow! You're too much!" exclaimed Misty. "You can have the Cascadebadge to show you beat me!" Ash then learned that his Pokémon that knew the Cut maneuver could now use it

Name: Staryu™
Number: 120
Type: Water

Chapter 5 All Aboard!

whenever he wanted. Misty also gave Ash TM11; this machine would allow him to teach one of his water-type Pokémon—when he got one—how to use Bubblebeam.

Name: Starmie™
Number: 121
Type: Water/Psychic

Before doubling back to Vermilion City to face Lt. Surge, the Vermilion City Gym Leader, Ash healed his Pokémon at the Pokémon Center in Cerulean City. From the nearby Mart, Ash stocked up on additional Poké Balls and Potions.

Once he was safely back in Vermilion City, Ash had Charmer Cut down the bush blocking the route to the Gym. Inside the large Gym, Ash was greeted by a trainer who was standing between two large pillars.

"Lt. Surge has a nickname. People refer to him as the Lightning American!" the trainer explained. "He's an expert on electric Pokémon! Birds and water Pokémon are at risk! Beware of paralysis too! Lt. Surge is very cautious! You'll have to break a code to get to him!"

Ash was challenged by three trainers who were hanging out at the Gym: Rocker, Sailor, and Gentleman. Fighting these trainers gave Ash good practice for his upcoming rumble with Lt. Surge.

Before facing Lt. Surge, Ash ran out to the Pokémon Center to heal his Pokémon. He returned to the Gym ready to go, but found the Gym Leader was guarded by a locked door. So this was the code he had to break!

Rocker told Ash, "When you open the first lock, the second lock is right next to it!" Ash also learned that failing to open the second lock immediately would cause the first one to reset. He searched for the two switches, which were hidden under two of the fifteen trash cans in the room. After trying several combinations, he managed to unlock the door.

"Hey, kid! What do you think you're doing here?" demanded Lt. Surge. "You won't live long in combat! That's for sure! I tell you kid, electric Pokémon saved me during the war! They zapped my enemies into paralysis! The same as I'll do to you!" declared the Gym Leader, who then released a Level 21 Voltorb, a Level 18 Pikachu, and then a Level 24 Raichu.

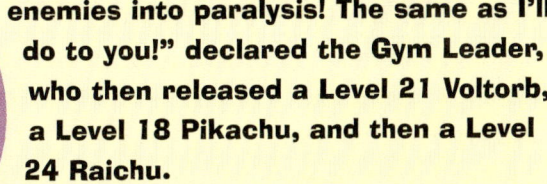

Name: Voltorb™
Number: 100
Type: Electric

Name: Raichu™
Number: 26
Type: Electric

Ash found that electric-type Pokémon, like his Pikachu, were particularly strong against Lt. Surge's Pokémon. Lt. Surge had high-level

Ash meets Lt. Surge in the Vermilion City Gym.

Chapter 5 All Aboard!

Pokémon, but they were nothing Ash's Pokémon couldn't handle.

Beating Lt. Surge earned Ash the much-coveted Thunderbadge, his third Pokémon Trainer's Badge. "The Thunderbadge cranks up your Pokémon speed! It also lets your Pokémon fly any time," Lt. Surge informed him. "You're special, kid! Take this!" Lt. Surge handed Ash a TM24, which Ash used to teach Pikoo, his electric-type Pokémon, the Thunderbolt attack.

In addition to the three Pokémon Trainer's Badges, Ash had already captured 13 Pokémon and had gathered information about 45 different types of Pokémon in his Pokédex. His next objective was to visit Celadon City and challenge Erika, the Pokémon Leader who specialized in Grass-type Pokémon.

Even though Ash knew that Celadon City had a Department Store with a huge selection of useful items for Pokémon Trainers, he didn't miss the chance to stop at the Vermilion City Mart for Super Potions to keep his Pokémon strong during battle.

Ash checked out his Town Map; he could take Route 11, but it was blocked by a sleeping Pokémon. He could take Route 6, but Ash suddenly saw a way to capture the Wild Pokémon he'd missed earlier on his journey—and find even more.

Backtracking a bit, Ash traveled through Diglett's Cave, which ended on Route 2 just after Viridian Forest. He headed north to Pewter City, then traveled along Route 3, again passed through Mt. Moon, and took Route 4 to

Cerulean City. At this point, Ash headed across Route 9 and through the dangerous pitch-black areas of Rock Tunnel, where he relied on the Flash technique to light up the path ahead. From Rock Tunnel, he traveled along Route 10 and quickly reached Lavender Town.

During this leg of Ash's journey, his favorite Pokémon, Charmer, reached Level 36 and evolved into a Charizard, which allowed it to learn Slash, an extremely powerful move that would allow Charmer to defeat many of its rivals with a single attack, yet receive no damage itself!

Name: Charizard™
Number: 6
Type: Fire/Flying

The areas Ash traversed on his way to Lavender Town were loaded with Wild Pokémon, so Ash used up many Poké Balls. Once he had captured one of the different types of Wild Pokémon from each area, Ash sped up his journey by using Repels to temporarily prevent Wild Pokémon attacks.

As Ash approached Lavender Town, he thought about the scary rumors he'd heard about the town's Pokémon Tower. Could the tower really be haunted? Luckily, Ash had read his Pokémon magazines and knew he shouldn't bother exploring the tower until he'd gotten his hands on a Silph Scope, which he could only find somewhere in Celadon City.

Lavender Town turned out to be much smaller than the other towns and cities Ash had been to thus far. It had a Pokémon Center and Mart, but what set it apart from other towns was the large Pokémon Tower.

Making his way among the few buildings in town, Ash spoke with several of the local residents. One person told him,

Chapter 5 All Aboard!

"This town is known as the gravesite of Pokémon. Memorial services are held in Pokémon Tower." Another person explained, "Ghosts appeared in Pokémon Tower. I think they're the spirits of Pokémon that the Rockets killed."

> **"Ghosts appeared in Pokémon Tower. I think they're the spirits of Pokémon that the Rockets killed."**

In one of the smaller buildings, Ash found an older man sitting at a table. "Hello! I am the official Name Rater!" the stranger said. "Want me to rate the nicknames of your Pokémon?" Ash showed each of the Pokémon he was carrying to the Name Rater, who commented on his Pokémon's names and gave Ash the chance to rename them.

Ash also encountered several people at the Volunteer Pokemon Center who were worried about their friend, Mr. Fuji, who seemed to be missing.

Ash's current plan involved traveling Route 8 to find the underground path that would lead him to Route 7 and on to Celadon City. Before setting out, Ash dropped into the Mart to pick up some Great Balls, Super Potions, Revives, Super Repels, and an Escape Rope.

Pathways to Adventure

Name: Vulpix
Number: 37
Type: Fire

Along Route 8, Ash was attacked by several new types of Pokémon, including a Vulpix, Ninetales, Growlithe, and an Arcanine. Charmer's Slash attack quickly defeated the Pokémon trainers who challenged Ash. By avoiding their line of sight, Ash even managed to sneak past several trainers without engaging in battle.

Before he could get to the underground path Ash needed to take to Route 7, Ash was confronted by Gambler. This trainer used two Level 22 Poliwags, followed by a Level 22 Poliwhirl, in a failed attempt to stop Ash from entering the building. Ash's Pokémon beat Gambler's Pokémon with relative ease.

Name: Ninetales
Number: 38
Type: Fire

Name: Growlithe
Number: 58
Type: Fire

The short trek along the underground path was uneventful. When Ash climbed up the exit ladder, he found himself a few paces away from Celadon City, the largest place he'd visited thus far. Here he knew he'd find a huge Department Store that

Name: Arcanine
Number: 59
Type: Fire

Chapter 5   All Aboard!

Name:
Poliwag™
Number: 60
Type: Water

was chock full of items that every Pokémon trainer wanted to get their hands on, the Gym where Erika was the highly respected Gym Leader, and much more!

Name:
Poliwhirl™
Number: 61
Type: Water

Ash could hardy wait to begin his exploration!

Ash's first stop in Celadon City was its largest building: the Department Store, where Pokémon trainers could shop for all sorts of useful goodies. The friendly young woman behind the counter in the main lobby of the store greeted him.

Ash can purchase many useful items from the Department Store.

According to the sign on the right edge of the counter, Ash was standing on the first floor near the Service Counter. The store had five floors and a rooftop. To the right of the counter was a staircase, on the left was an elevator.

Ash walked up the stairs to the second floor, which turned out to be the Trainer's Market. Here Ash bought various TMs from the two salespeople behind the counter.

The Third Floor was the TV Game Shop; several Super NES systems were set up so shoppers could check out the hottest new games. Ash didn't have time to play video games, so he traveled to the Fourth Floor where Wiseman Gifts were sold. The salesperson at the counter showed him a variety of different items, many of which couldn't be found anywhere else in the world.

Ash purchased a Poké Doll and then hiked up to the Fifth Floor, where he could purchase some useful power-up items, but the prices were extremely high. Ash made his way to the rooftop floor and surveyed the variety of vending machines there. He purchased three Fresh Waters, a Soda Pop, and a Lemonade. These drinks could replenish some of his Pokémon's HP or could be given away as gifts.

Now that Ash's inventory was full of handy new items, he decided to explore the rest of the city. He took the elevator back to the first floor and left the Store. His next stop, the Celadon Mansion, was interesting to wander around in but, other than finding a wild Eevee, there was little to do.

Name:
Eevee™
Number: 133
Type: Normal

Ash next spoke with several of the patrons in the Diner. He learned of a secret basement under the Game Corner, and a man sitting in a corner gave Ash a Coin Case so he could play the games at the Game Corner. In the building next to the Diner, he met a trainer who warned him, "Don't touch the poster at the Game Corner! There's no secret switch behind it!"

 "Don't touch the poster at the Game Corner! There's no secret switch behind it!"

Chapter 6 Fun 'n' Games Within Celadon City

Based on the hints he'd been given, Ash decided that the Game Corner should be his next stop. Even if he didn't find anything there, he could play the games. If he won enough coins, he could trade them in for various types of Pokémon at the Prize Exchange.

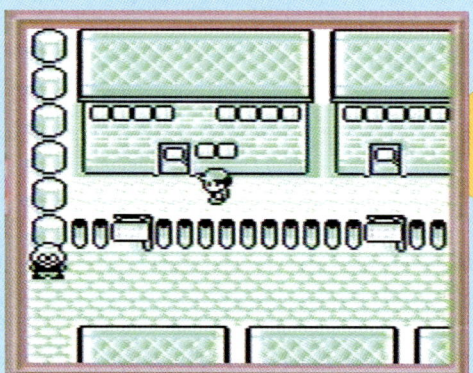

The Game Corner is a great place to hang out and play some games, but it's also a secret hideout for Team Rocket!

Ash walked into the Game Corner and strolled past the various game tables to the back of the room. He took a closer look at a person who was standing near a poster. It turned out to be a member of Team Rocket, who challenged Ash to a fight!

Charmer's Slash attack successfully beat the Team Rocket member's Level 20 Raticate and Level 20 Zubat. Before running off, the gangster said, "Our hideout might be discovered. I better tell Boss!"

Ash studied the poster the Team Rocket member had been guarding and discovered a hidden switch, which he activated. He figured the secret basement he'd heard about in the Diner would be a perfect place for Team Rocket's secret hideout, so he decided to investigate. After all, stopping Team Rocket from achieving its evil

Pathways to Adventure

goals was just as important as becoming a Pokémon Master.

He found a staircase that led downward and followed it to the basement, which turned out to have four levels. As he explored the maze-like area, Ash kept running into Team Rocket members, all of whom challenged him to fight. Finally, a Team Rocket member on the First Basement level told Ash, "Ok, I'll talk! Take the elevator to see my Boss!"

Ash found the elevator but couldn't make it move. It turned out that to make the elevator work he needed to find a special key that had been dropped by a guard somewhere in the basement. After a quick search, Ash found the key in the northwest corner of the Fourth Basement level.

On his way back to the elevator, Ash ran into a gangster. "Stop meddling in Team Rocket's affairs!" the gangster demanded, but then let it slip that the Boss had stolen the Silph Scope, and that it was hidden somewhere in the basement.

Back at the elevator, Ash used the special key, and then pressed the button that would take him to an as-yet-unexplored part of the Fourth Basement. When the elevator came to a stop, Ash found two guards blocking what looked like a large locked door. "How can you not see the beauty of our evil?" asked one of the guards, and attacked Ash with three different Pokémon. After Ash successfully beat the first guard, the second guard approached. "I know you! You ruined our plans at Mt. Moon!" he said just before he attacked Ash. As soon as Ash defeated this guard, the locked door opened to reveal a large room. Standing on the other side of two tables was a tall man named Giovanni; this was Boss, Team Rocket's notorious leader.

"So! I must say, I am impressed you got here," sneered Giovanni before launching his own attack using a Level 25 Onix, a Level 24 Rhyhorn, and a Level 29 Kangaskhan. Ash had Charmer mix its attacks, using Slash, Ember, and Scratch to beat its powerful adversaries.

Name: Rhyhorn™
Number: 111
Type: Ground/Rock

Soon the battle was over; Ash was once again victorious! "I see that you raise Pokémon with utmost care," observed Giovanni. "A child like you would never understand what I hope to achieve. I shall step aside this time! I hope we meet again." Giovanni, leader of Team Rocket, suddenly disappeared into thin air, leaving behind a Poké Ball. Ash grabbed it and discovered that it contained the Silph Scope, a high-tech device that could detect and identify Pokémon ghosts!

Name: Kangaskhan™
Number: 115
Type: Normal

Ash returned to the main floor of the Game Corner and left the building. His next stop was the Pokémon Center. After his Pokémon had been healed, Ash used the Center's computer to store some of his inventory items that he wouldn't be needing in the near future. He then proceeded to the southwest corner of the city, where the Celadon City Gym was located.

Pathways to Adventure

Inside the gym, several female trainers challenged Ash. "Hey! You are not allowed in here!" shouted one of the trainers before launching her attack.

Name: Gloom™
Number: 44
Type: Grass/Poison

After beating the second trainer, Ash had to chop down a bush that was blocking his path. He was immediately confronted by several more female trainers. Cooltrainer was the first in the group to challenge Ash with her three powerful Pokémon. Next up was Lass, who attacked Ash using two of her best Pokémon, a Level 23 Oddish and a Level 23 Gloom.

Name: Victreebel™
Number: 71
Type: Grass/Poison

As this battle was taking place, Erika, the Gym's Leader, watched Ash's fighting techniques with extreme interest. When she was up, she challenged Ash with a Level 29 Victreebel, a Level 24 Tangela, and a Level 29 Vileplume. At this point, Charmer had reached Level 42, so it easily beat these rival Pokémon with Slash and Scratch attacks.

Name: Tangela™
Number: 114
Type: Grass

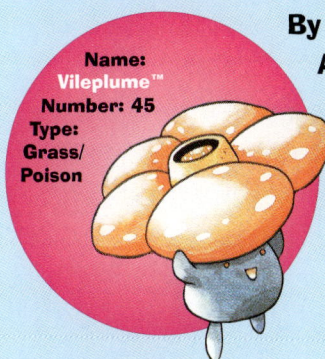

Name: Vileplume™
Number: 45
Type: Grass/Poison

By beating Erika, Ash received the Rainbowbadge and a TM21, which allowed him to teach one of his Pokémon the Mega Drain maneuver. "Half the damage it inflicts is

Chapter 6 Fun 'n' Games Within Celadon City

drained to heal your Pokémon!" Erika informed him. Ash now had four Pokémon Trainer's Badges!

It was now time to make the return trip to Lavender Town to check out Pokémon Tower, the massive, seven-story building that was believed to be haunted. Ghosts would be a new challenge! Ash also hoped to find the missing Mr. Fuji.

Returning to Route 7, Ash followed the underground path to Route 8, which led back to Lavender Town. Along Route 8, he trekked through the tall grass and caught some additional Wild Pokémon, including a Level 15 Vulpix.

Back in Lavender Town, Ash discovered that he could only get into Pokémon Tower through a dark cave in the northeast corner of town. In the tower's main lobby, several trainers were mourning the deaths of their favorite Pokémon. Ash took the staircase up to the second floor of the tower, and that's when things really started happening!

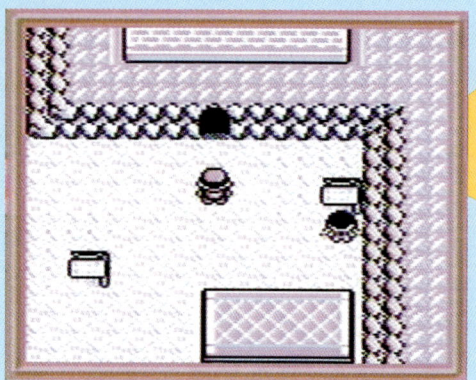

Ash locates the entrance of the Pokémon Tower and bravely goes inside.

On the second floor, Ash met up with Gary again. "Hey Ash! What brings you here? Your Pokémon don't look dead! I can at least make them faint! Let's go pal!" Gary's Pokémon, while numerous, weren't as well prepared for battle as Ash's. "You stinker! I took it easy on you!" cried Gary as his final Pokémon fainted. "How's your Pokédex coming, pal? I just caught a Cubone! I can't find the grown-up Marowak yet! I doubt there are any left! Well, I better get going! I've got a lot to accomplish. Smell ya later!"

Name: Cubone™
Number: 104
Type: Ground

Name: Marowak™
Number: 105
Type: Ground

Gary ran off toward the tower's exit. Ash walked across to the opposite wall and found the staircase to the third floor. Here he was met by a Channeler, who apparently thought Ash was an evil spirit and attacked him with a Level 22 Gastly. Charmer's Ember proved most useful against this ghostly Pokémon.

Leaving the Channeler behind, Ash walked across the room to the staircase up to the fourth floor. Another Channeler found Ash and challenged him. It was clear to Ash that to climb the tower's seven stories, he'd have to make it across the floors to each staircase, but the trick was getting past the Pokémon ghosts and the possessed people.

Name: Gastly™
Number: 92
Type: Ghost/Poison

Chapter **6** Fun 'n' Games Within Celadon City

On the fifth floor, a stranger walked up to Ash and intoned, "Give...me...your...soul..." and then attacked him, unsuccessfully of course, using a Level 23 Haunter.

Before ascending the next staircase, Ash noticed a strange pattern on the floor in the center of the room. When Ash stepped on these tiles, all his Pokémon were healed!

Name: Haunter™
Number: 93
Type: Ghost/Poison

Just as Ash was about to climb the staircase to the Seventh Floor, a large ghost appeared. Ash checked the Silph Scope and found out that this supernatural creature was a Level 30 wild Marowak! Ash commanded Charmer to use one Ember attack on this creature, and then he tossed a Great Ball at it. But the Marowak easily dodged the Great Ball. Ash realized that this creature couldn't be caught. It had to be defeated!

Ash finally reached the Seventh Floor of the tower, but there was no time to rest; three Team Rocket members were waiting for him. They attacked Ash one by one. "This old guy came and complained about us harming useless Pokémon! We're talking it over as adults!" the second gangster informed Ash before throwing out a Level 26 Koffing and a Level 26 Drowzee. "Pokémon are only good for making money!" he exclaimed. "Stay out of our business!" Ash

Name: Koffing™
Number: 109
Type: Poison

Name: Drowzee™
Number: 96
Type: Psychic

Pathways to Adventure

hoped that the old man the guard was talking about was the missing Mr. Fuji.

"You're not saving anyone, kid!" The third gangster warned before his four Pokémon attempted to defeat Ash. "You're not getting away with this!"

Finally, after all the Team Rocket members had been trounced, Ash was able to approach the man standing between two large statues, who turned out to be Mr. Fuji. "Heh? You came to save me? Thank you," Mr. Fuji said. "But, I came here of my own free will. I came to calm the soul of Cubone's mother. I think Marowak's spirit has gone to the afterlife," he continued. "I must thank you for your kind concern! Follow me to my home, Pokémon House at the foot of this tower."

Mr. Fuji and Ash were instantly transported to Pokémon House. Mr. Fuji then told Ash, "Your Pokédex quest may fail without love for your Pokémon. I think this may help your quest." He handed Ash a Poké Flute. "Upon hearing the Poké Flute, sleeping Pokémon will spring awake. It works on all sleeping Pokémon."

 "Your Pokédex quest may fail without love for your Pokémon."

Ash left Mr. Fuji's home and once again found himself standing in the heart of Lavender Town. He finally had time to assess what he'd picked up from the tower's floors:

Chapter 6   Fun 'n' Games Within Celadon City

Escape Rope, Awakening, HP Up, a Nugget, an X Accuracy, and a Rare Candy.

After a quick stop in the Pokémon Center, Ash set off toward his next destination: Saffron City.

Pokémon

CHAPTER 7

Team Rocket Invades Saffron City

Ash followed Route 8 once again, but this time passed by the entrance to the underground path. Shortly thereafter, he was halted at the entrance to Saffron City by a guard who complained that he was very thirsty. Luckily, Ash had stocked up on beverages in Celadon City.

"If you want to go to Saffron City, you can go on through. I'll share this with the other guards!" said the officer after taking the bottle of Fresh Water that Ash offered him as a gift.

Saffron City had quite a diverse population. Ash first visited Mr. Psychic, who gave Ash a TM29. This machine allowed Ash to give one of his Pokémon Psychic abilities, which could be used to lower an opponent's special fighting abilities.

The largest building in the city was the Silph Co. headquarters. This eleven-story building seemed quiet from the outside, but once Ash entered the lobby, he realized that members of Team Rocket were everywhere!

Silph Co.'s Corporate Headquarters

As Ash battled these gangsters, one by one, Charmer reached Level 46 and automatically learned the Flamethrower attack. To make room for this new attack, which caused most Pokémon to faint immediately, Ash had Charmer forget the less powerful Scratch attack.

Ash soon noticed the strange-looking tiles that were scattered around the floor of Silph Co. When Ash stepped on a tile, he was transported elsewhere within the building, but not, unfortunately, through locked doors. To get past some of these, Ash used the Card Key he had found hidden in a hallway on the Fifth Floor.

After much exploration and dozens of encounters with Team Rocket's most powerful and exotic Pokémon, Ash found Gary in a small room in the northwest corner of the Seventh Floor. "What kept you Ash?" asked Gary. "I thought you'd turn up if I waited here! I guess Team Rocket slowed you down! Not that I care! I saw you in Saffron, so I decided to see if you got better!"

The two rivals went at it again. After his five new Pokémon had been defeated, Gary said, "Well, Ash! I'm moving on up and ahead! By checking my Pokédex, I'm starting to see what's strong and how they evolve! I'm going to the Pokémon League to boot out the Elite Four! I'll become the world's most powerful trainer!" he bragged. "Ash, well good luck to you! Don't sweat it! Smell ya!" Gary stepped on a teleportation pad on the floor and disappeared.

Ash then teleported to the Eleventh Floor, hoping he'd finally find Giovanni there. "Stop right there! Don't you move!" shouted the gangster guarding the office of the Silph Co. president. The guard's three Pokémon—including a Level 32 Cubone, a Level 32 Drowzee, and a Level 32 Marowak—attacked Ash. Charmer's special fighting

abilities ran out of PP during the difficult battle, but luckily Ash had an Elixer and was able to replace 10 PPs of each of Charmer's abilities. After all of Charmer's special fighting moves were fully restored, Ash had no trouble beating the guard's Pokémon.

"So you want to see my Boss?" sneered the guard, but he allowed Ash to enter the office. As expected, Giovanni was inside. "Ah Ash! So we meet again!" he said. "The President and I are discussing a vital business proposition. Keep your nose out of grown-up matters. Or, experience a world of pain!"

Ash *had* to put a stop to whatever "business" Giovanni was conducting with the president of Silph Co. The company's Silph Scope was extremely useful for dealing with ghosts, so it made perfect sense that Team Rocket wanted control over this powerful technology. After all, their evil plan was to revive extinct Pokémon and use them for diabolical purposes.

The battle was joined. First, Giovanni tossed out a Level 37 Nidorino, which crumpled after a single Flamethrower attack. Next out was a Level 35 Kangaskhan; two Slash attacks, and this creature was down.

Name: Nidorino™
Number: 33
Type: Poison

The Team Rocket leader then sent out a Level 37 Rhyhorn, but by now, Charmer had reached Level 50. All it took was a Flamethrower attack, quickly followed by two Cut attacks, and the horned creature had passed out.

Now Giovanni's last hope was his Level 41 Nidoqueen. Two of Charmer's Slash attacks, however, quickly put an end to the battle.

"I lost again!" exclaimed Giovanni. "Blast it all! You ruined our plans for Silph! But, Team Rocket will never fall! Ash!" he commanded. "Never forget that all Pokémon exist for Team Rocket! I must go, but I shall return!" After his final threat, Giovanni vanished, leaving a very pleased Silph Co. president sitting behind his desk.

Name: Nidoqueen™
Number: 31
Type: Poison/Ground

"Thank you for saving Silph!" cried the relieved president. "I will never forget you saved us in our moment of peril! I have to thank you in some way! Because I am rich, I can give you anything! Here, maybe this will do!" He gave Ash a very special gift—a Master Ball. "You can't buy that anywhere! It's our secret prototype Master Ball! It will catch any Pokémon without fail! You should be quiet about using it, though."

 "Never forget that all Pokémon exist for Team Rocket!"

This was a prize worthy of a Pokémon Master!

Before Ash left the Silph Co. president's office, he used the computer to deposit several inventory items he no longer needed.

Chapter 7   Team Rocket Invades Saffron City

Now that the world was safe from Team Rocket—at least for the time being—Ash could again focus on his second goal: that of becoming a Pokémon Master. Ash's next step in this direction was to challenge this city's Gym Leader; much to Ash's surprise, it turned out that Saffron City had *two* Gyms, one larger than the other.

Ash discovers that Saffron City has two Gyms.

He chose to enter the smaller building first. Ultimately, he was searching for Sabrina, the city's Gym Leader, who was an expert at training psychic-type Pokémon.

She wasn't in the smaller Gym; instead, Ash was challenged by five trainers who specialized in martial arts and fighting-type Pokémon. Ash faced each of these trainers one at a time.

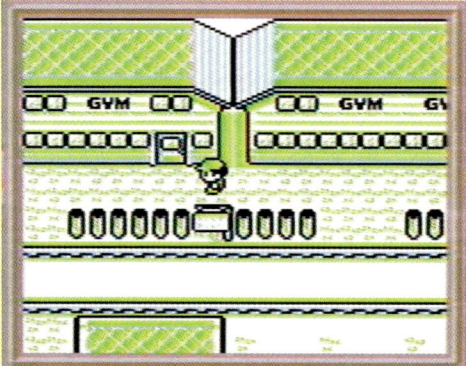

Name: Hitmonlee™
Number: 106
Type: Fighting

"I am the Karate Master!" declared the fifth trainer, who was standing next to two Poké Balls. "I am the Leader here! You wish to challenge us? Expect no mercy!" The Karate Master, Blackbelt,

challenged Ash using a Level 37 Hitmonlee and a Level 37 Hitmonchan.

Name: Hitmonchan™
Number: 107
Type: Fighting

When Charmer had defeated these two tough Pokémon, Blackbelt accepted his loss. "Indeed, I have lost! But, I beseech you, do not take our emblem as your trophy! In return, I will give you a prized fighting Pokémon! Choose whichever one you like!"

Ash chose the Poké Ball on the left, which turned out to be a Level 30 Hitmonlee. "You want the hard kicking Hitmonlee?" asked Blackbelt. "Yes," Ash answered. After adding this new Pokémon to his collection, Ash made for the city's Pokémon Center.

With his Pokémon once again fighting fit, Ash prepared for his fight with Sabrina. Because she trained psychic-type Pokémon, Ash was sure her Pokémon would use the Confuse technique, which could cause his Pokémon to hurt themselves. Thinking ahead, Ash visited the city's Mart and stocked up on power-ups that would revive the HP of his Pokémon during battle. If worse came to worst, he knew he could always change Pokémon during a fight if one became too confused and began to harm itself.

Ready to roll, Ash returned to the second Gym. He knew that Sabrina, holder of the Marshbadge, would be there.

The first thing Ash noticed about the Gym was the teleportation tiles on the floor and the layout—the Gym was made up of many small rooms. Just finding Sabrina was going to be tricky!

Chapter 7   Team Rocket Invades Saffron City

As Ash teleported from room to room, he was challenged by trainers who were working out in the Gym. As he fought these trainers, Ash was careful not to use up the PP for Charmer's most powerful specialty fighting techniques, the Flamethrower and Slash attacks. Just as in Pokémon Tower, Charmer's Ember attack worked particularly well on ghosts.

Finally, in a medium-sized room with only one teleportation tile, Ash found Sabrina. She assured him that she had seen his arrival in a psychic vision and began her challenge with a Level 38 Kadabra, followed by a Level 37 Mr. Mime, a Level 38 Venomoth, and a Level 43 Alakazam.

Name: Kadabra™
Number: 64
Type: Psychic

Kadabra quickly fainted when confronted with Charmer's Flamethrower, and just one of Charmer's Slash attacks did Mr. Mime in. Venomoth could only take an Ember and a Cut, but it was able to poison Charmer before it fainted. Instead of wasting time on an Antidote during battle, Ash had Charmer defeat Alakazam with two Flamethrower attacks. He then healed his prize Pokémon. That had been some battle!

Name: Mr. Mime™
Number: 122
Type: Psychic

"I'm shocked!" exclaimed Sabrina, who clearly hadn't seen her defeat in a psychic vision. "A loss is a loss. I admit I didn't work hard enough to win! You earned the Marshbadge! The Marshbadge makes Pokémon up to level 70 obey you! Stronger Pokémon will

Name: Venomoth™
Number: 49
Type: Bug/Poison

Pathways to Adventure

become wild, ignoring your orders in battle! Just don't raise your Pokémon too much!" Sabrina warned as she handed Ash the Marshbadge.

"Wait, please take this TM with you!" Sabrina then said. "TM46 is Psywave! It uses powerful psychic waves to inflict damage! Everyone has psychic power! People just don't realize it!" She then sent Ash on his way.

Name: Alakazam™
Number: 65
Type: Psychic

To get out of the Gym, Ash kept stepping on teleportation tiles until he reached the Gym's lobby. Now that he had five Pokémon Trainer's Badges in hand, plus several very powerful Pokémon, Ash was ready to face almost any challenge!

Ash's next stop was Fuchsia City. Here he would challenge the city's Gym Leader, Koga, to win the Soulbadge. Ash checked his town map and decided to return to Lavender Town and then take Route 12 to Route 13. He'd then follow Routes 14 and 15 to Fuchsia City.

Route 12 was composed of many docks with water on either side. This provided an excellent opportunity to catch some water-type Pokémon—all he had to do was move close to the water and use the Old Rod. Along the way, he was forced to defeat several Pokémon trainers who were trying to catch their own water-type Pokémon.

About two-thirds of the way down Route 12, Ash's progress was blocked by a sleeping Pokémon. Ash took the Poké Flute out of his inventory and began to play. As expected, the sleeping Snorlax woke up, but it attacked Ash in a grumpy

Chapter 7   Team Rocket Invades Saffron City

rage. Once Ash managed to calm the Snorlax down by defeating it, he sent it off into the mountains and continued onward into the Sport Fishing Area.

Name: Snorlax™
Number: 143
Type: Normal

Stopping inside a hut, Ash met a friendly man who handed him a Super Rod. This rod could be used for catching more exotic types of water-type Pokémon. "Use the Super Rod in any water! You can catch different kinds of Pokémon!" promised the fisherman. "Try fishing wherever you can!" Ash tried his new Super Rod out immediately and was rewarded by a Level 15 Goldeen!

Route 12's Sport Fishing Area is the perfect fishing spot for capturing exotic water-type Pokémon.

After what seemed like a very long walk, Ash approached a sign that read, "Route 13 North to Silence Bridge." Besides the eleven trainers who picked fights with Ash, his trek along Route 13 was uneventful. After making his way through some sort of a maze, Ash got onto Route 14 and then 15. Here he encountered additional trainers who wanted to practice their Pokémon fighting techniques. In this way, Ash slowly progressed toward Fuchsia City.

Pathways to Adventure

POKÉMON

CHAPTER 8

Hunting Season at the Safari Zone

By the time Ash reached Fuchsia City, all his Pokémon had received a good workout, so the first thing Ash did was visit the Pokémon Center and heal his Pokémon. That taken care of, he decided to check out the city's tourist attractions.

Inside the Fish Farm, Ash met the Fishing Guru's older brother, who gave him a Good Rod. Using this fishing rod, Ash was able to catch even more types of water-type Pokémon. Ash tried out his new rod in the Fishing Guru's backyard pond with good results.

Ash next visited the warden of the Safari Zone, who was in the building next to the Fish Farm. Unfortunately, this man had lost his gold teeth somewhere in the Safari Zone, so Ash couldn't understand a word he was saying.

Ash next decided to drop into the city's Gym and challenge Koga, the Gym Leader. This Gym appeared simple enough; it was a large room with two pillars near the entrance. The man standing next to one of the pillars called out, "Yo! Champ in making! Fuchsia Gym is riddled with invisible walls! Koga might appear close, but he's blocked off! You have to find gaps in the walls to reach him!" This was going to be a bit tricky!

Ash slowly made his way through the invisible maze, fighting each of the trainers he encountered, until he finally reached Koga. In a futile attempt to stop Ash, Koga released a Level 37 Koffing, a Level 39 Muk, another Level 37 Koffing, and finally a Level 43 Weezing. Using Charmer, Ash crushed Koga's Pokémon one by one. "Humph! You have proven your worth! Here! Take the Soulbadge!" boomed Koga.

"Now that you have the Soulbadge, the Defense of your Pokémon increases! It also lets you Surf outside of battle!" Koga informed him. "Ah! Take this too!" he added, and handed over a TM06. This TM contained Toxic. "It is a secret technique over 400 years old! When afflicted by Toxic, Pokémon suffer more and more as battle progresses! It will surely terrorize foes!"

Name: Weezing™
Number: 110
Type: Poison

Name: Muk™
Number: 89
Type: Poison

Ash meets Koga, the Fuchsia City Gym Leader.

After all his hard work, Ash was ready for some fun, so he headed for the Pokémon Paradise Safari Zone. According to a villager in front of the Safari building, Safari Zone had

Chapter 8 Hunting Season at the Safari Zone

81

a zoo in front and a Safari Game for catching Pokémon out back.

 After all his hard work, Ash was ready for some fun, so he headed for the Pokémon Paradise Safari Zone.

Ash went inside the Safari Game Pokémon-U-Catch building. The person behind the left counter asked Ash if he was a first-time visitor. "Yes," he replied. The person behind the right counter then explained, "Safari Zone has 4 zones in it. Each zone has different kinds of Pokémon. Use Safari Balls to catch them! When you run out of time or Safari Balls, it's game over for you! Before you go, open an unused Pokémon Box so there's room for new Pokémon!"

Before things went any further, Ash ran out to the Pokémon Center. Using the computer there, he accessed his Pokémon Storage System and, using the Change Box option, chose one of the twelve boxes that wasn't yet filled with data he had already collected. Now he was ready to go on safari!

Back at the Pokémon-U-Catch building, the clerk on the right told him, "For just ₽500, you can catch all the Pokémon you want in the park! Would you like to join the hunt?" Ash replied "Yes!" and received 30 special Safari Balls. "We'll call you on the PA when you run out of time or Safari Balls!" the clerk promised.

Ash walked into the Safari Park's first zone and immediately came upon a Venonat. Ash tossed out a Safari Ball and captured this Pokémon with ease.

During his first trip into the Safari Zone, Ash managed to catch Exeggcute, Rhyhorn, Nidorino, and several other Wild Pokémon. Ash had so much fun, he paid the admission fee two more times so he could catch as many Pokémon as possible.

Name: Venonat™
Number: 48
Type: Bug/Poison

In Zone 3, Ash found a Secret House.

"Ah, finally. You're the first person to reach the Secret House! I was getting worried that no one would win our campaign prize. Congratulations! You have won!" cried the man inside the house and handed Ash the HM03. Ash used this HM to give his Goldeen the ability to Surf. If Ash was the first one to find the Secret House, maybe he was finally ahead of Gary!

Name: Exeggcute™
Number: 102
Type: Grass/Psychic

Continuing his search, Ash found the warden's missing gold teeth in Zone 3. He'd return them before leaving Fuchsia City and hopefully find out what the warden had to say.

When Ash had used up his third set of Safari Balls, he knew it was time to continue on his quest. First, he visited the warden and returned his teeth; the warden was so grateful, he gave Ash an HM04. This machine gave Ash the ability to teach his Pokémon Strength, which gave them the power to

Chapter 8 Hunting Season at the Safari Zone

move large and heavy objects. Then, leaving the Safari Zone behind, Ash dropped into the city's Mart and purchased 10 Ultra Balls and five Full Heals.

Ash's next destination was the Power Plant between Cerulean City and the Rock Tunnel. To reach it, he would first need to take Route 18, which would merge into Route 17 and then became Route 16. It was going be a very long journey, so Ash used his bicycle to make the trip easier. As Ash passed through the building that marked the end of Route 16, he found his path was blocked by a sleeping Pokémon! Ever resourceful, Ash used the Poké Flute to wake the sleeping Snorlax up.

Shortly after his Snorlax encounter, Ash discovered another Secret House, where he met a young girl. "Oh, you found my secret retreat! Please don't tell anyone I'm here," she begged. "I'll make it up to you with this!" She gave Ash the HM02, which he immediately used to teach his Pidgey how to Fly. By riding on the back of his flight-capable Pidgey, Ash could now quickly travel between cities and towns that were located far apart! What a wonderful world this was!

After much traveling, Ash finally made it to the Power Plant by using Surf to paddle along the riverbank. Here he managed to capture the very rare wild Zapdos with an Ultra Ball!

Name: Zapdos™
Number: 145
Type: Electric/Flying

Ash then used Fly to return to Fuchsia City; by a stroke of luck, he landed in front of the city's Pokémon Center. After healing his Pokémon, Ash headed south to the beach and swam along Routes 19 and 20. This was a chance to use his Pokémon's Surf capabilities.

Pathways to Adventure

At Fuchsia City's coast, Ash uses Surf to swim to Seafoam Island.

Along Routes 19 and 20, Ash was challenged by several trainers. He also swam into several wild water-type Pokémon, which he managed to catch with Ultra Balls. About halfway down Route 20, Ash reached the shore of Seafoam Island.

Seafoam Island was a five-level maze of tunnels, pathways, rivers, and caves. Even worse, many Wild Pokémon were loose on this island, and Ash was constantly under attack. Finally, Ash had to use his Max Repels so he wouldn't be harassed by so many Wild Pokémon.

There were many large white boulders on this island, often located near black pits. Ash quickly realized that to gain access to many of the island's underground areas, he'd need to use his Pokémon's Strength capabilities to push these boulders into the pits. Doing this caused the water currents to change direction in the underground areas, allowing him to travel deeper into the maze.

Chapter 8 Hunting Season at the Safari Zone

Getting through this island took a lot of patience! Ash knew that if he became frustrated, he could always use his Escape Rope to return to Fuchsia City, where he could start this portion of his journey all over again. But that wasn't something Ash wanted to do.

After what seemed like a *very* long time, Ash found the exit from the caves and was once again able to follow Route 20, using Goldeen's Surf capabilities, toward Cinnabar Island.

Once on Cinnabar Island, Ash visited the city's Pokémon Center and its Mart, and then dropped in to the Pokémon Lab to chat with the scientists working there. There he was given the opportunity to trade in his Pokémon fossil, Dome, and his Old Amber—an item he had picked up while exploring the building next to the Pewter City Museum—for prehistoric Pokémon that had been brought back to life. Ash's visit had yielded valuable information for his Pokédex—and valuable Pokémon for his collection!

Ash then poked around the city's Mansion and found a special key that would unlock the front door to the city's Gym—so off to the Gym he went. After pummeling several trainers, he met the Cinnabar Island Gym Leader, Blaine.

Blaine was the most talented Gym Leader Ash had ever met. Ash was faced with a Level 42 Growlithe, followed by a Level 40 Ponyta, a Level 42 Rapidash, and a Level 47 Arcanine. By defeating these creatures, Ash not only earned the Volcanobadge he so badly wanted, he also received a TM38, which allowed him to teach one of his Pokémon the Fire Blast maneuver.

Name: **Ponyta**™
Number: 77
Type: Fire

Pathways to Adventure

Ash was ready to leave Cinnabar Island. He rode Goldeen directly north along Route 21's watery path. With so many Wild Pokémon swimming around, Ash was quickly able to catch a few, but then used his Max Repels to move along unhindered.

Ash's journey had come full circle; at the end of Route 21, he found himself back home in Pallet Town! Of course, he dropped in on both Professor Oak and his mother.

Ash's return home would be a short one. His ultimate goal of becoming a Pokémon Master required him to leave his hometown and travel along Routes 22 and 23, to Victory Road, and on to Indigo Plateau, where Ash would have the opportunity to prove himself as a Pokémon trainer by going up against the Elite Four.

But first, Ash needed to win the Earthbadge from the Viridian City Gym Leader. This Gym had been locked the last time Ash had been in the city, but he'd heard that the Gym Leader had moved in again.

Getting to Viridian City was a snap, and Ash was now a pro at defeating the trainers who worked out at the various Gyms. The Gym Leader himself was a bit of a surprise; he turned out to be none other than Giovanni, leader of Team Rocket!

 Viridian City's Gym Leader turned out to be none other than Giovanni, leader of Team Rocket!

Chapter **8** Hunting Season at the Safari Zone

Ash returns to the Viridian City Gym to face Giovanni, the city's Gym Leader!

When he was finally face to face with Giovanni, Ash had to defeat this evil gangster's strongest Pokémon, including a Level 45 Rhyhorn, a Level 42 Dugtrio, a Level 43 Nidoqueen, a Level 45 Nidoking, and finally a Level 50 Rhydon.

Name: **Dugtrio™**
Number: 51
Type: Ground

Needless to say, Ash was mighty proud of himself when he won the eighth and final Pokémon Trainer's Badge by defeating Giovanni a third time! This victory sent Giovanni and his Team Rocket organization into hiding—hopefully for a good long time!

It was now time to prove himself to the Elite Four and earn the title of Pokémon Master. Ash left the Gym and headed for Indigo Plateau via Routes 22 and 23.

By this time, Ash had captured more than 50 different Pokémon. He had also gathered information about 126 species of Pokémon in

Name: **Nidoking™**
Number: 34
Type: Poison/Ground

Pathways to Adventure

Name: Rhydon™
Number: 112
Type: Ground/Rock

his Pokédex. All six of the Pokémon Ash was currently carrying were very strong—all were ranked over Level 30—but Charmer, at Level 77, continued to be Ash's prize Pokémon.

Ash's walk along Victory Road was a glorious one. As he passed through various checkpoints, he was asked to flash each of his Pokémon Trainer's Badges at the guards.

Only accomplished Pokémon trainers, like Ash, were allowed to proceed further.

Chapter 8 Hunting Season at the Safari Zone

Even along Victory Road, Ash encountered Wild Pokémon. One of the world's rarest Pokémon, a Level 50 Moltres, lived in this area. Ash knew he'd only get one chance to capture this Pokémon, so he was very careful to catch it when it suddenly appeared before him.

Name: Moltres™
Number: 146
Type: Fire/Flying

Ash paused in front of the building at the end of Victory Road long enough to read the sign in front of it: "Victory Road Game—Pokémon League." Upon entering, Ash found himself within a stone-filled, cave-like room.

To find the exit, Ash set about moving boulders onto the switches located on the floor. He unblocked pathway after pathway and finally found the teleportation tile that would get him out of the cavernous area.

Ash looked around; he had been teleported near the outer edges of Indigo Plateau. He followed the checkered floor past many stone pillars that had Pokémon statues mounted on them.

A man stepped through the front door of a nearby building and warned, "Yo! Champ in making! At Pokémon League, you have to face the Elite Four in succession. If you lose, you have to start all over again! This is it! Go for it!" A woman behind a counter just a few paces away offered to heal Ash's Pokémon before he faced the Elite Four. These battles were a big deal!

Pathways to Adventure

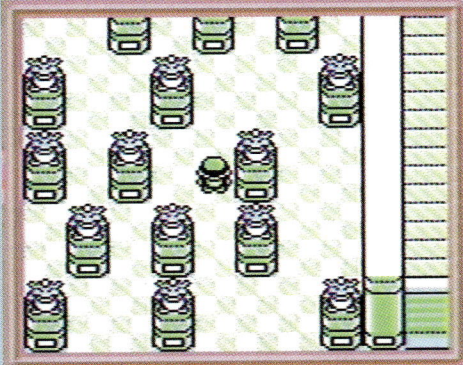

Ash navigates his way through a short maze of stone pillars.

 "If you lose, you have to start all over again! This is it! Go for it!"

To the left, Ash discovered yet another woman behind a different counter. She was selling useful items, such as Ultra Balls, Great Balls, Full Restore, Max Potion, Full Heal, Revive, and Max Repels. Ash took this opportunity to stock up on potions that would keep his Pokémon strong during the upcoming battles—Max Elixers or Max Ethers would be especially useful for insuring that none of his Pokémon ran out of PP during battle.

A trainer hanging out near the counter told him, "From here on, you face the Elite Four one by one! If you win, a door opens to the next trainer! Good luck!" Ash took a deep breath and walked through the nearby door. He found himself on a platform surrounded by water.

"Welcome to Pokémon League! I am Lorelei of the Elite Four!" declared an older woman who was standing on

the platform in front of a door. "No one can beat me when it comes to icy Pokémon! Freezing moves are powerful! Your Pokémon will be at my mercy when they are frozen solid! Are you ready?"

Lorelei, the first of the Elite Four to challenge Ash, releases five powerful Pokémon.

Lorelei released a Level 54 Dewgong, a Level 53 Cloyster, a Level 54 Slowbro, a Level 56 Jynx, and then a Level 56 Lapras. Charmer's Flame Blast worked well on Dewgong, and it took only one Flamethrower attack to bring Cloyster down. A single Flame Blast attack did the trick against Slowbro; to beat Jynx, Charmer used a Fire Spin. On Lorelei's final Pokémon, the Lapras, Charmer again used its Flamethrower attack. It worked perfectly!

Name:
Dewgong™
Number: 87
Type:
Water/Ice

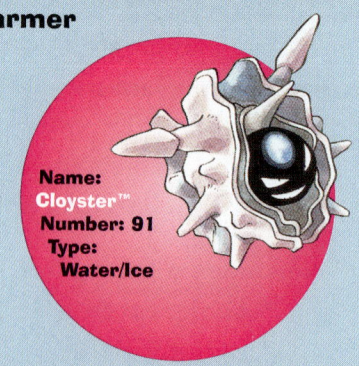

Name:
Cloyster™
Number: 91
Type:
Water/Ice

Lorelei had been soundly defeated in just a few minutes. "How dare you!" fumed Lorelei. "You're better

Name: Slowbro™
Number: 80
Type: Water/Psychic

than I thought! Go on ahead! You only got a taste of Pokémon League power!" The door behind Lorelei suddenly disappeared, and Ash walked through to another room.

Name: Jynx™
Number: 124
Type: Ice/Psychic

A man was waiting for him on the opposite side of the room, again in front of a door. "I am Bruno of the Elite Four!" he introduced himself. "Through rigorous training, people and Pokémon can become stronger! I've weight trained with my Pokémon! We will grind you down with our superior power!" he threatened with a laugh as he tossed his first Pokémon into battle.

Name: Lapras™
Number: 131
Type: Water/Ice

Bruno's best were a Level 53 Onix, a Level 55 Hitmonchan, a Level 55 Hitmonlee, a Level 56 Onix, and a Level 58 Machamp. Once again, Charmer used its most powerful fighting moves against Bruno's Pokémon. Ash was careful, however, to insure that the PP for Charmer's specialty moves didn't run out.

The battles were short and sweet. Ash was ultimately victorious! "My job is done!" stated Bruno, accepting his loss like a good sport. "Go face your next challenge!" The

Name: Machamp™
Number: 68
Type: Fighting

Chapter 9   A True Pokémon Master at Last

Ash takes on Bruno, the second of the Elite Four to challenge him.

door behind Bruno disappeared, and Ash proceeded forward.

"I am Agatha of the Elite Four!" this powerful Pokémon trainer said to Ash. "Oak's taken a lot of interest in you, child! That old duff was once tough and handsome! That was decades ago! Now he just wants to fiddle with his Pokédex! He's wrong! Pokémon are for fighting! Ash, I'll show you how a real trainer fights!"

Name: Gengar™
Number: 94
Type: Ghost/Poison

Agatha launched her attack against Ash using a Level 56 Gengar, a Level 56 Golbat, a Level 55 Haunter, a Level 58 Arbox, and a Level 60 Gengar. Ash retaliated with Charmer's Fire Spin and Flamethrower attacks, conserving the more powerful Fire Blast to use against only the most powerful of adversaries. Agatha kept her word; the battles against her Pokémon were very difficult. Charmer was even poisoned at one point! As before, Ash waited until he had

won the battle before spending the time to heal his prize Pokémon with an Antidote.

"Oh no! You're something special, child!" remarked Agatha after she, too, had been beaten. "You win! I see what the old duff sees in you now! I have nothing else to say! Run along now, child!" Before proceeding through the next door, Ash spent a few minutes healing his Pokémon with items from his inventory.

Name: Golbat™
Number: 42
Type: Poison/Flying

Name: Arbok™
Number: 24
Type: Poison

This fourth door led into a winding tunnel. Ash followed its curves to the room at the end; the moment he entered, the door locked behind him. He was trapped! With the last member of the Elite Four, no less!

"Ah! I heard about you Ash!" said this man. "I lead the Elite Four! You can call me Lance the dragon trainer! You know that dragons are mythical Pokémon! They're hard to catch and raise, but their powers are superior! They're virtually indestructible!"

Lance then demanded, "Well, are you ready to lose? Your League challenge ends with me, Ash!"

Although Lance used some very highly ranked and well-trained Pokémon—a Level 58 Gyarados, two Level 56 Dragonairs, a Level 60 Aerodactyl, and a Level 62 Dragonite—by this time Charmer had reached Level 79 and was incredibly powerful itself.

Pokémon

Ash is confronted by Lance, the leader of the Elite Four.

Name: Gyarados™
Number: 130
Type: Water/Flying

Ash's main trouble was with Gyarados; whatever Charmer dealt it, the Gyarados healed immediately! With persistence, Charmer was ultimately able to bring the creature down, but Ash quickly had to use a Full Restore to keep Charmer from fainting. Some of Dragonite's attacks were fierce, which kept Ash on his toes, but he was ultimately victorious thanks to his determination and skill.

"That's it!" cried Lance after the battle. "I hate to admit it, but you are a Pokémon Master! I still can't believe my dragons lost to you, Ash! You are now the Pokémon League champion! Or, you would have been, but you have one more challenge ahead. You have to face another trainer! His name is Gary! He beat the Elite Four before

Name: Dragonair™
Number: 148
Type: Dragon

Pathways to Adventure

you! He is the real Pokémon League champion!"

Name: Dragonite™
Number: 149
Type: Dragon/Flying

Ash wasn't surprised to hear that his lifelong adversary was about to challenge him once again, this time for the title of Pokémon League champion. Now, it was time to see who was really the best! Ash walked through the door behind Lance and into the room where Gary stood waiting.

"Hey! I was looking forward to seeing you, Ash!" said Gary. "My rival should be strong to keep me sharp! While working on Pokédex, I looked all over for powerful Pokémon! Not only that, I assembled teams that would beat any Pokémon type! And now, I'm the Pokémon League champion! Do you know what that means?" Gary taunted Ash. "I'll tell you! I am the most powerful trainer in the world!"

Name: Pidgeot™
Number: 18
Type: Normal/Flying

Gary was putting up a good show, but Ash wasn't fazed, even when Gary sent out six Pokémon. He started with a Level 61 Pidgeot, a Level 59 Alakazam, and a Level 61 Rhydon, and finished up with a Level 61 Exeggutor, a Level 63 Gyarados, and a Level 65 Charizard.

It took everything Ash had and all of his Pokémon's best fighting techniques to beat Gary, but Ash managed to do it!

"No!" cried Gary, when his last Pokémon, the Charizard, fainted. "That can't be! You beat my best! After all that work to become League champ, my reign is over already? It's not

Chapter **9** A True Pokémon Master at Last

fair! Why?" he moaned. "Why did I lose? I never made any mistakes raising my Pokémon. Darn it! You're the new Pokémon League champion! Although, I don't like to admit it."

Just then, Professor Oak ran into the room. "So, you won!" said Professor Oak to Ash. "Congratulations! You're the new Pokémon League champion! You've grown up so much since you first left with Charmander! Ash, you have come of age!" Ash had indeed accomplished quite a lot!

Turning to Gary, Professor Oak then said, "Gary! I'm disappointed! I came when I heard you beat the Elite Four! But, when I got here, you had already lost! Do you understand why you lost? You have forgotten to treat your Pokémon with trust and love!" he admonished his disappointed grandson. "Without them, you will never become a champ again!"

Professor Oak faced Ash once more and continued, "Ash! You understand that your victory was not just your own doing! The bond you share with your Pokémon is marvelous! Ash, come with me!" Ash followed Professor Oak into a nearby room.

 "Ash! You understand that your victory was not just your own doing! The bond you share with your Pokémon is marvelous!"

Pathways to Adventure

"Er-hem!" The Professor cleared his throat for this important moment. "Congratulations Ash! This floor is the Pokémon Hall of Fame! Pokémon League champions are honored for their exploits here! Their Pokémon are also recorded in the Hall of Fame! You have endeavored hard to become the new League champion! Congratulations, Ash, you and your Pokémon are Hall of Famers!"

Professor Oak then examined all of the Pokémon that Ash was carrying. He was most impressed with Charmer, but was very pleased at how well Ash had raised all his Pokémon. "Looking good! Go find my Aide when you get 150 Pokémon," the Professor instructed.

Name: Mewtwo™
Number: 150
Type: Psychic

Ash may have become a true Pokémon Master, but he had not yet caught all the different types of Pokémon still in existence, nor collected information on all the Pokémon ever, so his quest would continue. Ash now had to track down and catch the Pokémon that were missing from his collection; only then would his Pokédex be complete.

Now that Ash was a true Pokémon Master, Professor Oak told him about the Unknown Dungeon, a secret lair where Ash could find several very rare Pokémon, including a Mewtwo.

Very few Pokémon trainers had ever been to the Unknown Dungeon. To get there, Ash would need to take Route 24 back to Cerulean City and swim south until he reached the entrance to the dungeon's cave.

Chapter 9   A True Pokémon Master at Last

The World of Pokémon was now totally open to Ash. He could travel anywhere and would be respected by all. Now that Team Rocket's plans had been foiled, at least temporarily, Ash could spend as much time as he needed to complete the Pokédex and catch all the different types of Pokémon—all 151 of them! (*He* knew that there was a secret 151st Pokémon!)

Before Ash left Indigo Plateau, Professor Oak reminded him that to collect all of the Pokémon, he would have to trade Pokémon with other Masters.

No doubt about it, many more adventures were in store for Ash and his Pokémon!

And to Think Some People Collect Stamps.

OK, you've started collecting Pokémon™ and you're on your way to becoming a master trainer and you want to catch 'em all. How do you do it? Grab a Game Boy® Game Link® cable, grab a friend, hook up and start trading. It's that simple. So what are you waiting for?

"Got Ya!"

Get Connected And Collect Them All.

www.pokemon.com

Pokémon: © 1995, 1996, and 1998 Nintendo/CREATURES, GAME FREAK. ™ and ® are trademarks of Nintendo of America Inc. © 1999 Nintendo. Game Boy, Games and Link cable sold separately.

CATCH THE ADVENTURE FROM  VIZ

The hit TV series is now available on video and DVD!
3 episodes, 75 mins. each
$14.98 VHS/$24.98 DVD ea.

1. I Choose You! Pikachu!

2. The Mystery of Mt. Moon

3. The Sisters of Cerulean City

4. Poké-Friends

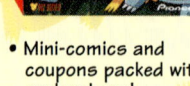
5. Thunder Shock!

- Mini-comics and coupons packed with each volume!
- "Pokémon is today's hottest cartoon."
  —Wizard Magazine

 **VIZ COMICS** — All-new comic book adventures of Ash, Misty, Pikachu and more!
b&w, 32-48 pages each, $2.95~$4.50 ea.

The Electric Tale of Pikachu

Pikachu Shocks Back

- America's #1 B&W Comic
- "Loads of fun; a rich fantasy with loads of appeal for both boys and girls."
  —Comics Buyer's Guide

VIZ GRAPHIC NOVELS

The Electric Tale of Pikachu

The original hit series in one handy collection, featuring 4 bonus color pages!

b&w plus 4 color pages, 160 pages,
August 1999
$12.95

To Order Call Viz Shop-By-Mail at (800) 394-3042
Fax (415) 546-7086 • Internet www.j-pop.com
Or call (888) 266-4226 for the location of a comics store near you